SURVIVING
the
CRISIS

You Survived!

Nathan

2004

SURVIVING
the
CRISIS

Bishop Neil C. Ellis

LEGACY
PUBLISHERS INTERNATIONAL

SURVIVING THE CRISIS
ISBN 1-880809-91-5
Printed in the United States of America
Copyright © 2004 by Neil C. Ellis

Legacy Publishers International
1301 South Clinton Street
Denver, CO 80247
Phone: 303-283-7480   FAX: 303-283-7536

Library of Congress Cataloging-in-Publication Data Pending

DEDICATION

This book is dedicated to:

My faithful and devoted wife of more than twenty years, Patrice Michelle, who has taught me how to live and how to love

The pastoral and administrative staffs of the Mount Tabor Full Gospel Baptist Church who have helped to lighten the burden of the pastorate, enabling me to do other things that God has assigned to me

The officers and members of the Mount Tabor Full Gospel Baptist Church whose inspiration has given me the impetus to dare such an assignment and who have shown more interest in my preaching and teaching of the Word of God than I ever had the right to hope for

Contents

INTRODUCTION

In recent years I can't help but notice that many Christians are struggling with things they should not be struggling with and spending a great deal of their time and spiritual energies rebuking the devil for things he has absolutely nothing to do with. Although it is true that each of us faces his or her own daily crisis, there are trials, or tests, that we must all face if we are to make progress toward the destiny God has for us, and no amount of prayer, fasting, or rebuke can change that fact. Such tests are sent by God Himself, and they are for our benefit. Why would we want to avoid them, escape them, or pray them away? These crises are God-sent.

There is a process that is necessary for making progress in our lives, and most of us are not happy with that process. With our modern mentality, we would like to jump from Point A directly to the prize without having to pay the necessary price and without having to suffer any of the pain associated with spiritual achievement. But if we are not willing or able to go through the required process, then there can be no progress for us. That's all there is to it.

There are also thorns in the flesh that God sends our way to keep our feet on the ground, to prevent us from becoming unduly exalted and losing the prize. No amount of prayer can turn these "thorns" away until they have served their purpose, so any attempt on our part to send them away prematurely is an exercise in futility.

So what is the purpose of affliction? Of hardship? Of want? Of opposition? Of persecution? Of need? Why does a loving God permit these things to hinder the lives of His children? Or are they hindrances at all?

If some bad things that happen to us are actually permitted by

God for our good, how can we know when a thing is from God and when it is from Satan? How can we know when to embrace a negative circumstance or when to rebuke and overcome it? These are all important questions, ones that have plagued Christians for many centuries, and I hope to answer them in the pages that follow.

My prayer is that those who pick this book up and read may be richly rewarded with truths that will enable them to stop struggling with the inevitable and to get busy with the process necessary toward progress, that they may find within these covers keys to overcoming every trial that life throws their way, and that in the end, they are able to say to their neighbors, friends, co-workers and relatives, "Come and see what the Lord has done for me. I have learned the secret of *Surviving the Crisis.*"

Bishop Neil C. Ellis
Nassau, Bahamas

Make a joyful shout to God, all the earth!
Sing out the honor of His name;
Make His praise glorious.
Say to God,
"How awesome are Your works!
Through the greatness of Your power
Your enemies shall submit themselves to You.
All the earth shall worship You
And sing praises to You;
They shall sing praises to Your name."   Selah

COME AND SEE the works of God;
He is awesome in His doing toward the sons of men.
He turned the sea into dry land;
They went through the river on foot.
There we will rejoice in Him.
He rules by His power forever;
His eyes observe the nations;
Do not let the rebellious exalt themselves.   Selah

Oh, bless our God, you peoples!
And make the voice of His praise to be heard,
Who keeps our soul among the living,
And does not allow our feet to be moved.
FOR YOU, O GOD, HAVE TESTED US;
YOU HAVE REFINED US AS SILVER IS REFINED.
YOU BROUGHT US INTO THE NET;
YOU LAID AFFLICTION ON OUR BACKS.
YOU HAVE CAUSED MEN TO RIDE OVER OUR HEADS;
WE WENT THROUGH FIRE AND THROUGH WATER;
BUT YOU BROUGHT US OUT TO RICH FULFILLMENT.

I will go into Your house with burnt offerings;
I will pay You my vows,
Which my lips have uttered
And my mouth has spoken when I was in trouble.
I will offer You burnt sacrifices of fat animals,
With the sweet aroma of rams;
I will offer bulls with goats.   *Selah*

COME AND HEAR, all you who fear God,
And I will declare what He has done for my soul.
I cried to Him with my mouth,
And He was extolled with my tongue.
If I regard iniquity in my heart,
The Lord will not hear.
But certainly God has heard me;
He has attended to the voice of my prayer.

Blessed be God,
Who has not turned away my prayer,
Nor His mercy from me!   Psalm 66

PART I

THE PROCESS FOR PROGRESS

CHAPTER 1

THE MAKING OF THE PROCESS

The man began to prosper and continued prospering, until he
became very prosperous.   Genesis 26:13

Those who want to become successful and make progress in their
lives need to prepare themselves for the journey, or, better said,
for the process. There is a process that is necessary to any progress,
and the process involves surviving any number of crises that come
our way.

I'm often amazed at the number of believers in the Body of Christ
who seem totally unaware of the fact that God designed our walk
with Him, our life in Christ, to be an abundant and progressive
experience. The apostle John wrote to the churches of his day:

> *Beloved, I wish above all things that thou mayest prosper and*
> *be in health, even as thy soul prospereth.*   3 John 2, KJV

This single verse of scripture makes clear the fact that not only
does God desire that our lives be prosperous, but also that there is
a progressive nature to the destiny that lies in store for us. If we are
willing to engage ourselves in the process of spiritual growth, there
is an unlimited horizon before us.

Many believers seem to think that the blessings of God will simply fall into their laps without them having to expend any real effort,
and when they have experienced a small, or introductory, measure

of success, they automatically assume that they have arrived and begin to "kick back" and beat their chests. Such a mindset only leads to stagnation and an inability to maintain what has already been obtained.

In speaking of the prosperity of Isaac, Genesis gives us a wonderful biblical description of God's intentions for all of us, His plan that we experience progress. Isaac *"began to prosper,"* then he *"continued prospering,"* and the end result was that *"he became very prosperous."* He *"began,"* but he also *"continued,"* and the eventual outcome was what we all desire—and what God desires. But it didn't happen overnight, and it didn't happen without struggles or challenges. As Isaac moved through the process necessary for progress, his victory came.

> *It didn't happen overnight, and it didn't happen without struggles or challenges.*

Since everything in the Bible is given to us for example, let us now follow the great patriarch as he pressed his way through every hindrance to his ultimate destiny, and let us be inspired to discover and fully engage ourselves in our own process for progress.

It's a process, and beginning the process is an important element, but it isn't everything. Beginning doesn't assure a good conclusion. The secret of Isaac's ultimate prosperity was that he *"continued."* He not only began the process, but he continued the process until the desired result was reached. So, what was the process?

It would be easy to read verse thirteen of this chapter and come to the conclusion that this whole process was easy. But if we read the first twelve verses of the chapter, we can quickly realize that it was anything *but* easy. Isaac had to face many challenges to get to verse 13 and to become *"very prosperous."*

But that's okay. Challenges don't change God or His desires for us. He has promised us victory—regardless of any challenges we might face along the way. For us, challenges just represent opportunities to move forward, and without them we would remain stagnant in our Christian experience. As we are presented with each of life's challenges, we then have opportunity to grow spiritually.

Growth is a process, and each of us must accept individual responsibility for our own growth, our own progress. Making an excuse that you have not grown and progressed because someone did not do something for you is unacceptable. There is no one responsible for your progress but YOU.

You can't blame the government, the church, your parents, or your friends. If your spiritual life has stagnated, it's YOUR fault. Why are so many people sitting back waiting for someone else to make things happen for them? You have God, so who else do you need? He said that YOU could do *"all things"*:

> *I can do all things through Christ who strengthens me.*
>
> Philippians 4:13

YOU can do it, and you can do it *"through Christ."* Start making an effort to help yourself, and He will help you. Stop waiting around for some miracle to drop out of the sky, and start making something happen. Stop waiting on Sarah and Susan, Jeffrey and Jimmy. God wants YOU to do it. Cut your own path. Blaze your own trail. Do something for yourself, and God will be there to help you.

God promised Abraham that he would be *"heir of the world"* (Romans 4:13), and that promise was passed down to his offspring (Isaac among them), but Abraham had to make it happen, and Isaac had to do the same.

The Bible is filled with promises that God made to many people in many periods, but He didn't just go around giving stuff away. Every promise was accompanied by a challenge, and if the person receiving the promise did not get up and make the effort to move through the process, nothing came of the promise.

Every man and woman in the Bible faced the same truth: there is a process necessary to personal progress, and a promise without the necessary process remains nothing more than a promise. That's all it can ever be.

Through His Word, God has made many promises to each of us, but we must now carve out our own process for progress on our way to the possession of the promises. Otherwise, the only thing we will be able to declare as Christians is that God has made us a whole lot of promises.

For those who haven't yet realized it, you can't just sing your way to promises fulfilled or testify your way to promises fulfilled. You can't even pray your way to promises fulfilled. There is a necessary process, and you must work your way through that process, if you want to make the desired progress.

As I have moved about the nations preaching the Gospel, I have observed that many people have their "Church stuff" together, but they're not making much progress in their personal and professional lives. They can tell you what the Lord said, what the latest dream is and what they see as its interpretation. They even seem to have the latest revelation, but why is it that they can't seem to make any progress in the things that really matter in their daily lives?

When these people talk, they have to talk about what is happening in their church, because that's all they have to report. Nothing of consequence is happening in their homes or their businesses. Nothing is happening where it really counts. By talking about what is happening in the church they can connect themselves to a corporate progress, but personally they have little to say, because in their personal lives there is little progress.

What God is doing in the Body of Christ as a whole is wonderful, but the most important thing in your life is your personal testimony. What is God accomplishing in YOU? Are YOU making progress by applying the necessary process? If not, you need to get busy.

Amazingly, many Christians are not prepared to face any challenges at all in their personal lives. They have somehow adopted the mistaken notion that once a person comes to Christ, all troubles cease. God will do everything for them, they believe, so they don't have to do anything for themselves. "God will make a way," they say, as if saying it resolves everything.

Well, God does make a way, but then you have to walk in it. God has destined you for great things, but you won't just get there automatically without any effort on your part. If you get there, it will be because you honored the process and continued in it until the desired result was obtained.

Some of us have a glimpse of the great destiny God has ordained for us, but He will not just transport us there on some magic carpet. He gives us a prophetic word, a dream, or a vision, and through this revelation He lets us glimpse the glory ahead. But, at the same time, He sets a course for our lives, and He expects us to follow that course. Whether we follow it to its logical conclusion is entirely up to us.

God gives us instructions, directions for progress, but many of us don't follow them carefully. We somehow have been duped into believing that because God is so good, He will give us what He has promised regardless of what we choose to do with the opportunities placed before us. Then, when we don't get to where God wants to take us, we tend to want to blame Him or His people or someone else. But we have no one to blame but ourselves.

I am doing everything I can these days to separate myself from those who want everything for nothing and to associate more and more with progressive people. If I intend to live a progressive life, then I must fellowship with progressive people. If we hang around unprogressive and unproductive people long enough, their spirit may jump off on us.

God is expecting you to make progress in your life. He took Joseph out of the pit and set him on his way, but Joseph had to do the rest. Our God is ready to lift you up out of life's pits too, but unless you are prepared to go through the process for progress, that's as far as you'll get.

It's true that we cannot extricate ourselves from Satan's pits, and so God does that for us. He will do what He is anointed to do, and then you must do what you are anointed to do. And prayer and fasting and worship—as good and as important as they are—will not accomplish the progress you desire. These form a very necessary part of your spiritual life, and I'm not "knocking" them, but I'm saying that if all you do is pray and fast and worship, you'll never make progress in your personal life. There are things that God will do for you, and then there are things that you must do for yourself.

I wouldn't want to minimize in any way the role that God, the Omnipotent One, plays in our Christian experience. We would be nothing without Him. But He will not do *everything* for us.

For instance, when people lie about us, we can pray, "God, stop the lies," but that won't necessarily stop them. You have to face the lies, maintain your dignity and victory, and move forward anyway.

That's exactly what happened to Joseph. God took him out of the pit, but He didn't stop people from persecuting him, lying about him, and causing a scandal that tarnished his good reputation. And God didn't keep evil men from throwing Joseph in prison. All of this was part of the process, so praying that it would go away wouldn't have helped.

These circumstances, as terrible as they must have seemed at the time, were not about to go away. Instead, Joseph had to learn to maintain his integrity through the persecution, the lies, the scandal, and the imprisonment, and to be spiritually on top of things so that when he was called upon by the reigning pharaoh, he would have an answer for the problems of Egypt. When Joseph got to that point, by working through the process, then he was ready to rule, and God exalted him to be prime minister of Egypt.

Until he got to that point, Joseph was anointed to face lies and persecution and keep on going, and he had to know that God had a purpose in every part of the process. If he had failed to continue pressing forward at any point, he could have lost his great destiny.

Your process may be very different than Joseph's and very different than mine. God tailor makes a process specifically suited to our particular needs. He doesn't have to do for you what He does for me, and I may not have to go through what you have to go through. We are all individuals, and God handles us on an individual basis.

> *He had to know that God had a purpose in every part of the process.*

This requires us to maintain an intimate personal relationship with the Lord and a daily walk with Him. He reserves the right to give us each individualized instructions, and we must be keen enough in the Spirit to receive them.

Instead of drifting through this Christian life, you need to start paying attention. Instead of trying to imitate other Christians (who may well have gotten their specific instructions from God), you need to find His specific will for YOU. It is not wrong to be inspired and encouraged by the experiences of others, but if you try to mimic them, you will soon find that your results are not identical with theirs. And they may be far from it. There is no guarantee.

Live out your own destiny. There is something unique that God has placed in you that the world desperately needs and awaits. Don't bury what's in *you* by spending your lifetime trying to be like someone else. Walk in your personal anointing.

Genesis 26 has much to say about this required process for progress:

> *There was a famine in the land, besides the first famine that was in the days of Abraham. And Isaac went to Abimelech king of the Philistines, in Gerar. Then the Lord appeared to him and said: "Do not go down to Egypt; dwell in the land of which I shall tell you. Sojourn in this land, and I will be with you and bless you; for to you and your descendants I give all these lands, and I will perform the oath which I swore to Abraham your father. And I will make your descendants multiply as the stars of heaven; I will give to your descendants all these lands; and in your seed all the nations of the earth shall be blessed; because Abraham obeyed My voice and kept My charge, My commandments, My statutes, and My laws."*
> *So Isaac dwelt in Gerar.*   Genesis 26:1-6

It was a time of famine, and we should note first of all that when you begin your process toward personal progress, things may get worse before they get better. That's just how the process works.

Sometimes, just before God opens the windows of heaven and pours you out a blessing, it will seem that every door has closed to you, and that there is famine in your life. At times, it will seem that there is no one who can help you, and there's a purpose in that too. When you do begin to make progress under these difficult circumstances, you'll know that it is not being accomplished in your own strength, but that it is because of your Lord working in you.

There are many people like Abraham, I believe, whose promise of blessing is so great that it will outlive them, carrying over to succeeding generations. Still, none of those generations will get a free ride. God will require of them, as He did of Isaac when he followed his father Abraham, that they make their own commitment.

The Lord appeared to Isaac in Gerar. We can always expect the Lord to speak to us in times of crises. He will not necessarily get us out of that particular crisis, whatever it happens to be, but He will show us what to do *in* the crisis. He gives us guidelines, principles, or instructions that we can follow. This is the process through which our deliverance can come.

If God were just to deliver us from every crisis, we would learn nothing from the experience. Some people are spiritual parasites, always tugging on God for a little blessing. He wants us to learn from our process so that we can then be strong enough to help to bring deliverance to others.

When the Lord spoke to Isaac in Gerar, He warned him not to go into Egypt (a type of the world), but to live in the place He would show him. Abraham had gone to Egypt under very similar circumstance (see Genesis 12:1-10). In his day, there had also been a famine, and when Genesis 26:1 speaks of *"the first famine that was in the days of Abraham,"* it is referring to that very famine, which was said to be *"severe"* (Genesis 12:10).

Going to Egypt at such a time was not at all unusual. It was considered the wise thing to do. In time of famine, whole families packed up their things and moved to the safety of Egypt until the famine had passed. But God's people are not to do what is normal or expected. They take their cue from above, not from what is acceptable to others. This particular famine had come as a curse upon unbelievers, and if God's people followed the unbelievers, they would be following the curse.

Start taking your cues from the Lord, and stop listening to every Tom, Dick, and Harry that comes along. Don't automatically do what everybody else is doing. Let others do what they will, but you must listen to what God is telling *you* for *your* life. Stop repeating what everyone else is saying, and start speaking what God is saying to you personally.

Since what God is preparing you for is not normal, but extraordinary, He may well require of you more than the normal. You may even consider what He requires of you to be extraordinary, but don't be surprised by it. If God is suddenly requiring more of you and asking you to do things you've never done, take it as a good sign. He is preparing you for something new. From that moment on, every time you go to the House of God, expect to hear something new from Him.

> *Since what God is preparing you for is not normal, but extraordinary, He may well require of you more than the normal.*

Whatever you do, don't try to put God in a box and limit Him. You cannot predict how and when He will speak or act. He wants to surprise you. He also wants to disturb your mind and conscience with what He says, so if what you hear hurts, that's even better. It may hurt for the moment, but it will help you in the long run.

If God is preparing you to be a channel of blessing to coming generations, He will do it in the way He sees best. It will not happen as it has in former times. Let Him be God. Isaac was not to do what his father had done. Abraham had gone to Egypt, but Isaac was not to go there.

This must have been a very difficult moment for Isaac. He revered his father, and naturally would have done as his father had done before him. But God was saying not to do it, so he must know that God had a purpose. And if he wasn't to go to Egypt, where should he go? God spoke to him again and told him to stay right where he was. That was clear enough, and Isaac obeyed.

It is a mystery to me why Christians the world over have to struggle so with whether or not to obey God. God's way is the way of blessing, and Egypt's way is the way of cursing. That's not much of a choice, the way I see it.

Surprisingly, many Christians choose to disobey, and then they ask God to bless them—in their disobedience. That takes a lot of nerve. When we willingly defy the explicit instructions of the Lord, how can we then expect Him to bless us?

God's command to Isaac carried at least seven special blessings. He said: (1) *"I will be with you,"* (2) *"I will ... bless you,"* (3) *"To you and all your descendants I will give all of these lands,"* (4) *"I will perform the oath which I swore to Abraham your father"* (Genesis 26:3). (5) *"I will make your descendants multiply as the stars of the heaven,"* (6) *"I will give to your descendants all these lands,"* and (7) *"In your seed all nations of the earth will be blessed"* (Genesis 26:4). Following God always has many known and unknown benefits.

There are always choices involved in the making of the process, and if we want to make progress, we cannot afford to follow the crowd. We must pay attention to what God has said and what He is currently saying, and then we must obey Him. He presents us with the choices, and then He stands back to see what our decision will be. If we obey, there is a resultant blessing, and if we disobey, there is a resultant penalty. But it's up to us which we receive. Isaac chose to stay in Gerar and be blessed.

It is time that we all began to walk in total obedience to the Word of God, and the next chapter will aid us in our understanding of that all-important subject. These are all steps necessary for *Surviving the Crisis.*

CHAPTER 2

OBEDIENCE ALWAYS PAYS

Then Isaac sowed in that land, and reaped in the same year a hundredfold; and the Lord blessed him.   Genesis 16:12

"Isaac sowed in that land." Which land was that? It was Gerar. And what was going on in Gerar at the time? There was a famine. Talk about crisis ... . Isaac had a very big one on his hands.

Isn't it interesting that Isaac was led to sow in a land that was currently experiencing famine. Does that even make good sense? Would anyone in their right mind do a thing like that? Well, Isaac did, and the results were astonishing.

God often asks His children to do things that seem out of the ordinary, and even without logical explanation. If you haven't yet had this experience, you will. If you are serious about your relationship with God, He will come to you at some point and challenge you to do something that may make absolutely no sense to anyone else—not even to you.

When God does this, be careful. This is not a game. If God asks you to do the unusual, He is preparing you for unusual blessings. And when they come, He will be glorified, for there will be no other explanation.

When Isaac did the unthinkable, sowing in a time of famine, something wonderful happened. He didn't go broke or have to declare bankruptcy. Instead, he reaped *"in the same year,"* and he reaped *"a hundredfold."* What year was that? It was the year of the famine.

Where did he sow? He sowed in Gerar, a land that was experiencing famine. And yet he reaped, he reaped in that same year, and he reaped a hundredfold.

There was no logical explanation for this. God blessed Isaac because of his obedience, and everyone saw it and understood it. Gerar was the last place anyone would have thought to sow at the moment, but God told Isaac to do it, he did it, and he was blessed.

If you find yourself in the midst of some crisis, know that God wants to demonstrate His power in that crisis and get glory for His name. You may suffer as others for a time and be tempted to compromise as others do, but blessings are coming. Just remain faithful.

Abraham had been permitted to go to Egypt, but going to Egypt would not have been acceptable for Isaac because he had specifically been told *not* to go. Most of us like to hear God say, "Go," but His "stay" is just as important and should also be welcomed. Sometimes He says to us, "Stand still." That's a hard command for many to obey, but if God is telling us to stand still, He must have something important to show us right where we are at the moment.

As we saw in Chapter 1, God made seven promises to Isaac, and these would all be his if he was willing to *not* do what others were doing. These blessings would not only enrich Isaac, but would also lift up his children and grandchildren. This is what we have come to call a generational blessing, and it is given to those who go to extraordinary lengths to obey God.

Isaac not only stayed in the land of famine (no doubt opening himself up to the criticism that he was putting his entire family at risk), but he also did something even more bizarre—he sowed in the dry fields of that land. But Isaac did this because God had told him to do it, and that makes all the difference. We sometimes do stupid things because we're not thinking right, but obeying something that God tells us to do is never a stupid thing to do, and the results are always obvious to everyone.

This is why I have such a low level of tolerance for compromise when it comes to obedience to God and His Word. God's Word is not open to discussion, and it needs no adjustment from us. If God said it, let's get busy doing it. Period.

When God has showed me something, I don't care how ridiculous it might appear to others. I trust God enough that I would never risk missing His blessing for something a man has said. I get started doing it—whatever it is.

How can we work together with God unless there is mutual trust? We must trust Him implicitly, and He must be able to trust us, that we will do what He says. So before God can take us to new levels in Him, we need new levels of trust, and we need to demonstrate new levels of trustworthiness to Him. God doesn't bother to speak to those who never do what He urges them. Instead, He goes in search of those whom He knows *will* obey.

> *We must trust Him implicitly, and He must be able to trust us, that we will do what He says.*

Many of the things God tells us to do are His way of testing us to see if we are willing and obedient. When He knows that our hearts are in the right place, then He can show us the really important things. And, just as Isaac was challenged to do what his father had not done, even now, in this new age, God is dealing with us on a very different level. He is calling us to be forerunners, those who experience a thing for the very first time.

As we do things on God's behalf that don't seem to make sense in the eyes of some—whether Christian or non-Christian—we prove once again that standing on God's Word works. Obedience to Him always pays off. When He tells us to do something and we do it, the results are always to our advantage. And when He tells us to refrain from doing something and we obey, we are always glad we did. Isaac obeyed God, and his reward was that he reaped bountifully.

Some seem to be trying to buddy up to God to see what handouts they can get. That's not what God is looking for in us. He is looking for obedience. You don't need to make deals with God to get what you want. Just trust Him and do what He says.

When Isaac, out of obedience to God, did something unusual, God did something unusual for him in return. It was Isaac's obedience that caused him to reap. And his reaping was totally miraculous. He reaped from parched land, he apparently reaped out of season, and he reaped a hundredfold—an amazing return.

The scriptures emphasize the fact that Isaac *"reaped in the same year."* Evidently this means that he should not have been expecting a crop so soon. God brought the crop in ahead of time, and He did it from parched soil.

The greatest miracle may have been the size of the harvest. Farmers always hope for a good crop, but *"a hundredfold"*? That's unheard of.

I must pause here to interject another very important principle, one that is important to our future financial prosperity. The best time for us to sow finances into the Kingdom of God is in a time of famine, when we can least afford it. Such a sowing in faith brings a quick and bountiful harvest.

Sometimes when you are sick and need a physical healing, you can sow a seed into the Kingdom on behalf of your sickness. When you sow, put a name on your seed. Call it Healing. And sow something serious. A one-hundred-dollar offering given by a person who has access to millions is not a serious offering, because it will hardly be missed. Sow something more serious. A good guideline is this: The seed you sow must affect what you have in order for you to reap what you need. Since the seed you are sowing is being given to help you meet your need, sow out of your need, and sow in proportion to your need.

Obedience Always Pays

In the case of a person whose marriage is in danger of failing, set aside a seed, first naming it Healing for My Marriage, and then sow that seed where God shows you. For the person who needs a home, why not sow a seed into someone else who needs a home desperately? You may have been saving for a down payment on your house. I challenge you to take a portion of that money you have set aside and sow it into a down payment for someone else. "Why in the world would I want to do that?" I imagine someone saying. Because when you sow in obedience out of your need, it is an unusual act, and God will reward you with an unusual blessing.

God didn't just bless Isaac; He blessed him *"a hundredfold."* When he was sowing into that parched ground, he must have felt like he was stretching himself, extending himself dangerously, but that's what we have to do when we expect a hundredfold blessing. If Isaac's venture had failed, he might have been wiped out. But when God is in it, we can't fail. When He has spoken, you can never go wrong. Your blessing is assured.

You may be so flat broke that you wonder how you can even sow, but if God is speaking to you to sow, you can count on a hundredfold blessing. And it will come to you quickly. Don't miss it.

Now, let's put this hundredfold blessing into context. If you were to sow ten dollars and reap a thousand dollars, that wouldn't help you much in today's economy. A thousand dollars doesn't go very far these days. But a hundredfold blessing means something much greater than that.

If you took an exam that had twenty questions on it, and you got them all right, you would get a mark of 100% on your exam. A hundredfold, or 100%, represents fullness, wholeness, completeness. When God gives you a hundredfold blessing it means that He has blessed you in every area of your life to the fullest extent. A hundredfold blessing fills you up in your finances, in your family life, in your health, in your faith, and in every other way. That's the kind of blessing we all need.

The hundredfold blessing never comes without sacrifice on our part, but when it comes it ensures that we can enjoy life to the fullest extent. God commanded His people through the prophet Malachi:

> *"Bring all the tithes into the storehouse,*
> *That there may be food in My house,*
> *And prove Me now in this,"*
> *Says the Lord of hosts,*
> *"If I will not open for you the windows of heaven*
> *And pour out for you such blessing*
> *That there will not be room enough to receive it."*
>
> Malachi 3:10

The hundredfold blessing never comes without sacrifice on our part.

But what benefit would it be to you to have a barn running over with produce and be too sick to enjoy it? What good would it do for a man to have plenty of money but suffer endlessly from a nagging wife? (Or for a woman to have access to money but suffer endlessly from a cheating husband?) How could you enjoy a big, beautiful home if, when night comes, you can't sleep? What joy could a fine house bring you if one of your children was on drugs and the other was in jail? In such a situation, your money would be going to lawyers or to compensate the victims of your children's crimes.

This is why the hundredfold blessing is so important. God wants to bless you and ensure that you enjoy His blessing to the fullest. His hundredfold blessing is for your love life, your prayer life, your business life, your family life, your educational life, and any other area that concerns you. God wants to bless you in every area of your life, and you can have such a blessing as you walk in total obedience to Him.

Verse twelve of Genesis 26 ends with these powerful words: *"The Lord blessed him."* What could this mean? Hadn't God already given him a harvest from parched land? And hadn't that harvest come unusually early? And hadn't that harvest been unusually large? What more could there be? And yet there was more.

After stating all of the other blessings, the verse ends with these words: *"The Lord blessed him."* There was more blessing, more than just material things, more than just physical bounty. The blessing for Isaac went far beyond the material. He was a truly blessed man. How awesome!

Isaac received what many are now calling a Jabez kind of blessing:

> *And Jabez called on the God of Israel saying, "Oh, that You would bless me indeed, and enlarge my territory, that Your hand would be with me, and that You would keep me from evil, that I may not cause pain!" So God granted him what he requested.*
>
> 1 Chronicles 4:10

"Bless me indeed." Oh, I like that.

It's time to put your relationship with God to the test. Ask Him today to bless you with health and wealth, to bless your marriage and your family life, to bless your career or business, to bless your many relationships, to bless your mind, your spirit, and your soul. Ask Him to bless you coming in and going out, in the field and in the city, when you are rising up and when you are sitting down. Tell Him that you need the hundredfold blessing to fall on you today. If, like Jabez, your heart is right, and you are asking for the right reason, God *will* respond.

As I grow older, I have found myself thinking more and more about the challenges of retirement and old age and have come to the conclusion that God doesn't want me to be dependant upon my children. They will have their own children to care for. It wouldn't be fair to them to have me solely dependent upon their care, as they will need to concentrate on raising the next generation. My conclusion is that God wants to meet all of my needs through a hundredfold blessing, so that I will be prepared for old age.

I have other desires that I'm believing God to fill in His hundredfold blessing on my life. I don't want to live out my latter years having someone else bathe me and dress me. I want to die with all my mental faculties in tact and with my physical body strong and fully functional. I would just like to fall asleep one day and wake up in the arms of Jesus.

Job shows us that we can *"declare a thing"* and *"it will be established"*:

> *You will also declare a thing,*
> *And it will be established for you;*
> *So light will shine on your ways.*   Job 22:28

This would be a good time for you to declare: Let the hundredfold blessing fall on me.

The Lord blessed Isaac, and this was nothing new, for He has never had a problem blessing His own. Blessing you is something He wants very much to do. Believe me.

Others may not be nearly as happy as you are about your blessing. The world (made up of the unsaved) does not take kindly to our blessings. We already have something they don't have—the joy of our salvation—so why should we also have material prosperity to boot?

The unsaved somehow believe that they should have the exclusive right to large bank accounts, houses, and yachts, and they are somehow disturbed when they see real Christians having not only the joy and peace they don't have, but also material possessions. Some people will begin to call you "materialistic" and will try to make you feel badly for being blessed. Because of this many Christians have shied away from material possessions, and the consequence is that God's favor upon His people has not been seen in the measure He would like for it to be seen.

It is time that we put a stop to this practice. Let saints everywhere realize that it glorifies God when they do well. So, may the blessing of the Lord upon His people be boldly displayed in the days ahead. It's time to let the world know that God has been good to us, and that His blessing is rich.

As we noticed in the previous chapter, the blessing upon Isaac was progressive. He *"began to prosper,"* then he *"continued prospering,"* and he did this until he *"became very prosperous"* (Genesis 26:13). This lets us know that God wants to take us from one level of blessing to another level of blessing, and there is always a new level awaiting us. By the time the devil "gets on your case" about all of the blessings you have been receiving on Level A, you can be moving up to Level B.

God told me one day that He wanted to give us a "You-can't-catch-up-with-me" blessing. I understood Him to mean that when people being used by Satan were about to execute their plan of attack against us, to discourage us, cut off our channels of blessing, and push us back, they would have to immediately regroup and lay new plans, because we would already be moving on to new things in God. Their plan would be designed for a certain level of blessing, and by the time they get ready to execute their plan, we have already moved on from that level to another level.

When Abraham was on his way to Egypt, he envisioned certain problems he might encounter there:

Now there was a famine in the land, and Abram went down to Egypt to sojourn there, for the famine was severe in the land. And it came to pass, when he was close to entering Egypt, that he said to Sarai his wife, "Indeed I know that you are a woman of beautiful countenance. Therefore it will happen, when the Egyptians see you, that they will say, 'This is his wife': and they will kill me, but they will let you live."

Genesis 12:10-12

When God blesses us, He does it openly, to provoke jealousy from the world. He not only blesses you, but He puts a kind of magnifying glass over your blessing, so that when the world sees the blessing, it looks even larger than it really is. Suddenly people think you are more blessed than you really are.

As Abraham was on his way to Egypt, he had this "you-can't-catch-up-with-me" blessing. It came because he had fully obeyed the Lord. And it came in a time of famine, just as Isaac's blessing did.

Suddenly Abraham noticed that everything around him had dried up. When such a thing happens to us, we often go into a state of depression. But we must not despair because of circumstances around us. We may be at the point of departure, ready to move forward into new blessings, and God may be preparing us for our final instructions. So, celebrate your dry seasons, because God has a purpose for them.

The point is that Abraham was obedient to God, and his obedience brought about prosperity:

Abram was very rich in livestock, in silver, and in gold.

Genesis 13:2

Isaac was also obedient to God, and he received a hundredfold reward. God's instructions to Abraham and to Isaac were different, but the requirement of obedience was the same for each. "If you do what I say, I will bless you," God told Abram. And His words to Isaac were the same. Obedience to God always pays off.

When Moses delivered the Law to the children of Israel, he concluded:

> *The Lord will again rejoice over you for good as He rejoiced over your fathers, if you obey the voice of the Lord your God.*
>
> Deuteronomy 30:9-10

That's the key: *"if you obey."* If you do what God says, even when you don't understand it, He will bless everything you touch. He will make you fruitful in every sense of the word. The book of Job agrees:

> *That's the key: "IF you obey."*

> *If they obey and serve Him,*
> *They shall spend their days in prosperity,*
> *And their years in pleasures.*
>
> Job 36:11

Obedience to God will cause you to spend your active years in prosperity and your old age in pleasures. Stop governing your life by what others are doing and start listening to God for His specific instruction for your life. And whatever God is telling you to do, just do it. Do it regardless of how crazy it may seem. Do it, even if you are in a time of famine. Trust God that He knows best and obey Him, and you will become a living witness that obedience to God always pays off. This is an essential step toward *Surviving the Crisis.*

CHAPTER 3

GET READY TO BE OPPOSED

For he had possessions of flocks and possessions of herds and a great number of servants. So the Philistines envied him.

Genesis 26:14

There is a downside, a drawback, a disadvantage, if you will, connected with progress, and it is that you will suddenly have many enemies. This fact presents to many a crisis they are unable to overcome.

As we have seen, God wants us to be ever moving forward, to be advancing, to be growing and maturing, to never be at a standstill. His will for us is progressive. The apostle Paul wrote of moving *"from glory to glory"*:

> *But we all, with unveiled face, beholding as in a mirror the glory of the Lord, are being transformed into the same image from glory to glory, just as by the Spirit of the Lord.*
>
> 2 Corinthians 3:18

Isaac experienced this when he *"began to prosper,"* then he *"continued prospering,"* and he did this until he *"became very prosperous."* In this way, he moved through the necessary process, and by moving through the process, he made progress in his personal life.

When the famine came to Gerar, where he was living, God told him not to do what everyone else around him was doing (fleeing to Egypt), but to stay right where he was and to sow in that parched land, believing for a miraculous increase. That's exactly what Isaac did, and God blessed him for it.

God had told him that if he was obedient, a sevenfold blessing would come upon him. Isaac loved God and wanted to do His will, and he also wanted God's blessings. But God was about to take him to a new level, and this required of him a new level of commitment.

God has gone on record about how He feels concerning the prosperity of His children. There can be no doubt. He wants to set us up as examples to the world. He wants to place us high on a hill for everyone to see. He takes delight in our prosperity. We are to be shining lights to others:

> *Let your light so shine before men, that they may see your good works and glorify your Father in heaven.* Matthew 5:16

We are to serve as a means of causing jealousy in the hearts of those who don't know God. They should look at us and say to themselves, "If that's what God does for those who trust and serve Him, then I want to know God too." Our daily lives should, in this way, be a living testimony to others.

God has destined us for a life filled with the extraordinary, the magnificent, the miraculous, that which is difficult to explain away. When God does for us something that we could have done for ourselves, no one considers that to be a miracle, or a blessing from God. His blessings are so extraordinary that we could not have received them in any other way.

There was a problem, and suddenly it's fixed. There was a situation, and suddenly it's resolved. People have counted us out, and suddenly we're up and running. One moment they are expecting us to breathe our last breath, and the next moment they see us looking stronger than ever before. Now that's a blessing, and when it happens, you will know it, and everyone around you will know it too.

When God told Isaac to stay put in a difficult situation and to sow in a parched land, it seemed like a ridiculous thing to do. But just believing in a God we can't see seems ridiculous to many. So, our very faith is often considered ridiculous, and certainly the process through which we are saved seems ridiculous to those who are yet outside of Christ.

So, why should we hesitate to do "ridiculous" things for God? He has done "ridiculous" things for us. Our very salvation through the shed blood of Jesus Christ is a blessing we find difficult to explain, but we know we have it. My entire life and ministry, my sole purpose for existence in this world, and everything I do and preach are all centered around the faith I have in a Person I have never shaken hands with. That surely must seem ridiculous to the world. Yes, you and I are quite qualified to operate on the level of "ridiculous" faith.

> *Just believing in a God we can't see seems ridiculous to many.*

Isaac did a ridiculous thing, investing his precious seed in a parched land, but he reaped, he reaped more quickly than expected, and he reaped much more than expected. Then his real problems began.

Isn't it interesting that as long as we are standing still, doing nothing with our lives, going nowhere, sitting in utter stagnation, and making no progress at all, no one bothers us or even pays attention to what we're doing. But the minute we begin doing something positive with our lives, enemies appear out of nowhere and begin to harass us. Most of us were better liked when we had nothing and were accomplishing nothing. We had fewer enemies when we were still in the world, and when we were broke, unproductive, and unprogressive.

When we were still drinking, smoking, and carousing at all hours of the night, we had more friends than we could count. But the moment we truly committed ourselves to Christ and it became clear that the Lord was blessing us, our so-called "friends" disappeared. They suddenly switched allegiances.

Most people find it easier to love us when they're doing better than we are. When we get to the place that we can help ourselves, and we no longer need them to survive, they suddenly lose their psychological grip on us, and we no longer have to make a mad dash every time they call. When this happens, these people suddenly and mysteriously move from our friends column into our enemies column.

You can count on this very thing happening in your life, because it's like a package deal. If you begin making progress in life, get ready for envy, jealousy, and strife to take hold of those around you. It's like clockwork. It never fails. The moment you begin to make progress expect your enemy count to go up fast. That's what happened to Isaac.

It is stated that the Philistines envied Isaac, but I'm convinced that others must have envied him too. What about all those who had fled to Egypt because of the famine? They would surely have resented the fact that Isaac stayed behind and prospered. The reason I can say this is that I have observed life as it is. It is a very normal thing for people to envy those who prosper.

Of course, neither the Philistines nor those who had fled to Egypt had a right to resent Isaac. They had not been willing to take the risks he had, to make the sacrifices he had, to obey God as he had, or to follow the process he had. They had no right to prosper, but they envied Isaac nevertheless—especially the Philistines.

These men never thought for a moment of asking Isaac what the secret of his prosperity was so that they could follow the process too and be blessed. They could only envy, nothing more. That's what enemies are like. They never seek to understand. They just hate to see you blessed. That's all. They're not concerned with what you had to go through or how much you had to sacrifice to get where you are today. They just hate it that you're doing so well.

But don't take it personally. Such hatred is really directed at God. It was God who had blessed Isaac, and God's blessing upon a person is always cause for jealousy and anger among those who don't know and love Him. God loved Isaac and blessed him, so the Philistines had to hate him and try to harm him in any way they possibly could.

Isaac worked hard to sow that difficult year, yet his enemies cared nothing for his toil and sweat and tears. They knew nothing of the inner struggles he had fought, and they would not have cared if they had known. All they saw was the results of his progress, and they couldn't deal with it. Isaac had obeyed God, and God had blessed him, and now men hated him because of it.

Don't expect everyone to be happy for you when the Lord blesses you, and don't expect everyone around you to help you celebrate. Don't even be surprised if someone in your family, your church family, or a co-worker on your job becomes annoyed over what God is doing in your life. So that this won't come as a shock, prepare your spirit for it now. Progress and envy go together. Get used to the idea.

Just as your life in God is progressive, the animosity it arouses in those around you will be progressive too. As you make personal progress, your list of enemies will grow, and the antagonism of people around you will escalate. The more you have to celebrate, the more you will have to fear from others. Your level of progress will determine your level of opposition. This is just as true for a professional career or a business career as it is for a ministry.

Jesus warned us to expect opposition:

SURVIVING THE CRISIS

So Jesus answered and said, "Assuredly, I say to you, there is no one who has left house or brothers or sisters or father or mother or wife or children or lands, for My sake and the gospel's, who shall not receive a hundredfold now in this time—houses and brothers and sisters and mothers and children and lands, with persecutions—and in the age to come, eternal life."
Mark 10:29-30

> These blessings will come "with persecutions."

First, Jesus spoke of the blessings that come to those who choose to sacrifice for His sake and for the sake of the Gospel. He promised them a hundredfold *"in this time,"* or in this lifetime. There's that hundredfold blessing again. It is complete and all-encompassing.

But Jesus didn't leave it there; there was more. These blessings will come *"with persecutions."* This word *persecutions* is plural. There will not be just one persecution. Every time God blesses you, there will be an accompanying response from your enemies. Each blessing will have a corresponding persecution. That's just part of the overall package.

If you don't want any more enemies, then you'll have to forsake all forward progress and remain stagnant. That's the only way the devil will leave you alone. If you remain stationary, your list of enemies will remain stationary too. But when you move, it will move too.

Your forward motion exposes the truth about many people around you. If you were to remain stagnant, you might never know their true character. It is your progress that brings it to the light.

If you choose to remain stagnant, you may think of people around you as being almost like family members. But move from one level to the next, and you will soon see who they really are. My wife and I have found this to be true in every level of our personal progress.

Get Ready to Be Opposed

At every level, our "close friends" count declined, and our "enemies" count increased. People—even many church people—hate it when you prosper. As you get excited about the prospects for progress, prepare your spirit, at the same time, for the negative reactions your progress will evoke in others.

When you notice that your enemy count is going up, it's a time for rejoicing. Praise God in that moment because it is an indication that you are making progress.

This problem of arousing the ire of others around us is so great that Jesus urged us:

> *Love your enemies, bless those who curse you, do good to those who hate you, and pray for those who spitefully use you and persecute you, that you may be sons of your Father in heaven.*
>
> Matthew 5:44-45

Now this teaching makes more sense to us. God's blessings upon us always wake up many enemies.

One of the reasons we bless our enemies is because they are signals to us that we're doing something right, and when the worst enemies show up, it's time for us to *really* rejoice. We have something to shout about. Our God is helping us to make progress toward our final destiny.

Please take time to thank the Lord for this. He is worthy of all of your praise. You may feel strange at first, thanking God for your enemies, but you'll get used to the idea.

The Philistines had shown a similar animosity toward Abraham, Isaac's father. After his death, they had gone about stopping up his wells, filling them with dirt:

> *Now the Philistines had stopped up all the wells which his father's servants had dug in the days of Abraham his father, and they filled them with earth.*
>
> Genesis 26:15

This may not mean much to some, but wells represented life in that part of the world, and they also represented ownership of the land. When the first well was dug on a given piece of land, it signaled to all that the person having the well dug was the rightful owner of the land. In their hatred, the Philistines just defied the existing laws of the land, ignoring the fact that the wells belonged to Abraham and filled them with "earth," or dirt. They were trying to deprive Abraham's descendants of their rightful heritage. If the truth were to be known, they would have killed Isaac if they could have.

When Jesus said that we should love our enemies, did He mean that we had to befriend them? Surely not. He said that we should love them, bless them, and pray for them, but that doesn't mean we have to invite them to sleep over at our houses. They just might take everything with them as they are leaving.

Your enemies want to destroy the mark of your ownership and rob you of all that God has given to you, but don't let them do it.

As you move forward, the lies will not stop, the resistance will not stop, the criticism will not stop. But please just keep going. Keep moving forward with the process, so that you can experience personal progress. None of us enjoys being hated and mistreated, but we have only two options. We can remain stagnant and experience more calm, or we can make progress and stir up dissent and strife. You make the choice.

The local Philistine king, Abimelech, tried to get Isaac to go away:

> *And Abimelech said to Isaac, "Go away from us, for you are much mightier than we."*   Genesis 26:16

Well, it certainly wasn't Isaac's fault that he was *"much mightier"* than the Philistines. It was God's blessing upon his life that made him mighty. Still, he decided to do as Abimelech requested. Gerar was a big place, and there was no reason to stay where he was not wanted. So Isaac moved on a little way and *"pitched his tent in the valley of Gerar, and dwelt there"* (Genesis 26:17). Rather than anger the local authorities, he decided to take the humble route.

For Isaac, Gerar represented the place of obedience, and he was not about to leave it. But for the sake of peace, he was now willing to move to a lower place. Sometimes obeying God seems to take you to your lowest point, and sometimes when you obey Him, as we have seen, it means that things will get worse before they get better.

Now, Isaac had to adjust to a new location and a new lifestyle. It was the difference between living on the mountain and living in the valley. Recognizing the tactic of the enemy, to cause friction by confrontation, he decided to avoid it. Obeying God always brings benefits, but walking in obedience can certainly take you to some low places, and, at times, even get you into troubling situations.

Once, when Jesus told His disciples to get into a boat and cross to the other side of the lake, and they obeyed Him, they were very surprised to encounter a terrible storm along the way. The Christian life is like that. It may seem that we have had life easy when we were in the world and that all hell has broken loose since we accepted Christ as Savior. But this is part of *"the deceitfulness of sin"*:

> *Exhort one another daily, while it is called "Today," lest any of you be hardened through the deceitfulness of sin.*
> Hebrews 3:13

Sin seems enjoyable and even helpful at first. It is only after we are deep in the clutches of the evil one that he begins to show us his true intention. And, in the same way that the life of sin deceitfully shows us its temporary side, the Christian life seems to be one battle after another. This is also a deceitful picture. There *are* battles, but we are always victorious and, more importantly, we win the final battle.

God allows the challenges that come into our Christian life to cause us to be totally dependant upon Him. We must not rely on flesh or our own devices, or we will surely go astray. Living a life of faith and obedience to God is no guarantee that things will always go smoothly, but we do reap some awesome rewards in the process.

Being a Christian seems to be especially difficult for our young people. They are just at that stage of their lives when they are ready to experience many new things, and, to them, saying "no" is one of the most difficult things imaginable. Their hormones are raging for release, and everyone around them seems to have someone to love, and they have no one. The first time someone looks at them longingly, they are hopelessly and incurably "in love." Then, of course, comes the demand to prove their love by physical acts.

These are not easy times for our young people, and they need our prayers. The enemy is determined to fill their wells with dirt and thus deprive them of their spiritual inheritance. At any age, it's not easy to live a progressive Christian life, but the benefits are wonderful, so it's well worth every challenge we may face.

Isaac was not discouraged by the violent actions of his Philistine persecutors. He decided to just redig the wells:

> *And Isaac dug again the wells of water which they had dug in the days of Abraham his father, for the Philistines had stopped them up after the death of Abraham. He called them by the names which his father had called them.* Genesis 26:18

Isaac refused to allow what his enemies had done to stop or hinder his level of progress. It wasn't worth it. He would just redig the wells. What the enemy had buried, he would uncover again. He also dug a well in the valley where he was now living:

> **Also Isaac's servants dug in the valley, and found a well of running water there.**   Genesis 26:19

The King James Version of the Bible calls this well *"a well of springing water."* Evidently it was a well fed by a spring near the surface of the land. Until that moment, the tactics of the Philistines had been to fill in the wells that had been dug, but now they encountered a problem. The water of this well was so close to the surface that it couldn't be stopped. Every time they attempted to fill it, the water would again bubble to the surface. This caused the Philistines to change their tactics. If they could not stop up the wells, then they would claim them as their own.

Isaac was not a quitter.

But Isaac was not a quitter, and he kept digging wells until eventually he had one that was not contested by the Philistines. How wonderful that must have been for him. He had outlasted his opposition, having been more stubborn than them all.

I'm sure that the enemy has tried to close up your wells, but if you will just hold steady and be faithful to God, you will soon experience a breakthrough that no one can stop. Suddenly, everything around you will begin to prosper in a way that is unstoppable. It will affect your marriage, your business, and every other area of your life.

Get ready for it, and get ready to be opposed at every level. Prepare your spirit to face many enemies. Always remember: God will not allow the enemy to have the last word in your life. You will win the final battle if you remain faithful to the Lord and to the process He has given you for progress in your personal life, ultimately *Surviving the Crisis*.

CHAPTER 4

WHEN YOU HAVE DONE
THE RIGHT THING

But the herdsman of Gerar quarrelled with Isaac's herdsmen,
saying, "The water is ours." So he called the men of the well
Esek, because they quarrelled with him. Then they dug another
well, and they quarrelled over that one also. So he called it's
name Sitnah. And he moved from there and dug another well,
and they did not quarrel over it. So he called its name Rehoboth,
because he said, "For now the Lord has made room for us, and
we shall be fruitful in the land." Genesis 26:20-22

As we have seen in the last chapter, after the servants of Isaac hit spring water in the Valley of Gerar and the Philistines could not close it up, they changed tactics. Now they claimed every well he dug as their own. If they could not block him one way, they would block him another. One very common tactic is to try to take from you the blessings God has heaped upon your life.

For Isaac, this represented a crisis of grand proportions, but he refused to get down and dirty with these people. Each time they took something from him, he just moved on and opened another well. This is important, but we will get to it later in the chapter.

Isaac gave names to each of the wells he dug, and each one had a special meaning. The final well, the one that was not contested by the enemy was named Rehoboth. That name literally means "spaciousness." *"Now,"* Isaac said, *"the Lord has made room for us."*

God is making room for you, and I know that this must be very good news. How do I know that God is making room for you? As I was writing this book, I heard the Lord say to me, "Tell the people that I'm making room for them." I'm not sure what that might mean to you individually, but I do know that God never lies and never fails to keep His promises.

Isaac now had an assurance that had to come from God: *"We shall be fruitful in the land."* You may be at the point of making a major decision that will affect the rest of your life. Many are thinking about moving on to some greener pastures. Let me remind you that God commanded Isaac to stay put, even when Gerar was experiencing famine. If you stay where God has planted you, you can proclaim with assurance: *"We shall be fruitful in the land."* That's His guarantee.

> *You may be at the point of making a major decision that will affect the rest of your life.*

At a later time, Isaac did make a move:

> *Then he went up from there to Beersheba. And the Lord appeared to him the same night and said, "I am the God of your father Abraham; do not fear, for I am with you. I will bless you and multiply your descendants for My servant Abraham's sake."*
> Genesis 26:23-24

God is preparing to do something so awesome for you that you just might be frightened by it. His word to you, as it was to Isaac, is *"Fear not,"* and His assurance is *"I am with you."* Get ready for blessing because God has said, *"I will bless you and multiply your descendants."*

When You Have Done the Right Thing

Knowing that God is with you and that you have nothing to fear is one of the major keys necessary for progress in your spiritual and material life. When God is with you, what can possibly harm you?

Joseph experienced this abiding presence of God in his life—even in his darkest moments:

> *Now Joseph had been taken down to Egypt. And Potiphar, an officer of Pharaoh, captain of the guard, an Egyptian, bought him from the Ishmaelites who had taken him down there. The Lord was with Joseph, and he was a successful man; and he was in the house of his master the Egyptian. And his master saw that the Lord was with him and that the Lord made all he did to prosper in his hand.* Genesis 39:1-3

> *So it was, when his master heard the words which his wife spoke to him, saying, "Your servant did to me after this manner," that his anger was aroused. Then Joseph's master took him and put him into the prison, a place where the king's prisoners were confined. And he was there in the prison. But the Lord was with Joseph and showed him mercy, and He gave him favor in the sight of the keeper of the prison.*
> *The keeper of the prison did not look into anything that was under Joseph's authority, because the Lord was with him; and whatever he did, the Lord made it prosper.* Genesis 39:19-21 and 23

What God is about to do in your life, will be so far beyond anything you have been expecting that, as I said earlier, it might shock and even frighten you. But you have nothing to fear, because God will be with you at every step of the way. Now, that *is* good news.

This is your ticket to progress. As long as God is with you, you will make progress. And He has promised never to leave you.

When God spoke to Isaac in Genesis 26:24 and said that He was with him and he need not fear anything, He said that He was doing it all *"for My servant Abraham's sake."* As we have seen, the great blessings God will soon pour upon you will benefit not only you, but also your children and your grandchildren, down to three and four generations. Long after you are already dead and gone, they will be reaping the rewards of your decision to faithfully follow Christ. Won't it be wonderful when the Lord says to your grandson, "I'm doing this for your grandfather's sake"? "Because he was faithful to Me, I will bless you. I promised him I would do it, and I never fail to keep My promises." Get ready for it.

Isaac was so grateful to God that he built an altar and gave thanks:

> *So he built an altar there and called on the name of the Lord, and he pitched his tent there; and there Isaac's servants dug a well.*   Genesis 26:25

Isaac didn't wait until he saw the increase before beginning to worship God. No sooner had God made a commitment to him than he was already building an altar of worship. Only then, after he had given due reverence to God, did he proceed to pitch his tent. And there also he dug another well.

Would this well attract enemies as before? Isaac had had so many bad experiences with the local tribesmen that he must have been holding his breath. Then, sure enough, one day a caravan appeared on the horizon, and no less than King Abimelech himself appeared. He was accompanied by a close friend and by the commander of his army. This did not look good, and Isaac and his people must have been tense as the party approached.

When Isaac confronted the Philistine king it was politely, but with firmness:

When You Have Done the Right Thing

"Why have you come to me, since you hate me and have sent me away from you?" Genesis 26:27

The answer was very interesting, to say the least:

"We have certainly seen that the Lord is with you. So we said, 'Let there now be an oath between us, between you and us; and let us make a covenant with you.' " Genesis 26:28

What was happening here? There had been a famine in the land, and Isaac had gone to live with the Philistine king Abimelech. Isaac had so prospered during the famine that it caused the Philistines to envy him, and Abimelech had urged him to leave them and move on. Now, the king is coming to him asking to make a covenant. In verse 16 Abimelech chased Isaac away, but now in verse 26, he comes in search for him. What had happened in the meantime? God had made room for Isaac and his party, and he had prospered so much that it was evident to everyone—even to a heathen king—that God was with him.

This is the reason we must not be disturbed by those who oppose us, count us out, or work against us. They might be running us off now, but one day they will come running to us when they need our help and they know that God is with us. Those who are trying to take advantage of you now will one day be offering you their blessings. Those who are lying about you now will one day sing your praises.

And there is nothing sweeter than seeing your former enemies changed into your best supporters and helpers. When those who have been trying to pull you down are suddenly building you up, you'll be mighty happy.

"Go away from us," Abimelech had said, but now he desired Isaac's

friendship. And your time is coming. Those who have hated you will one day seek your help. That's why I truly believe there has never been a more exciting time to be a Christian walking in obedience to God.

It was not Isaac's genius that changed his circumstances. It was the fact that God was with him, and this was evident to everyone—even the pagans around him. Now they realized that it would be in their best interests to make a covenant with Isaac.

What type of covenant was Abimelech interested in?

> *"That you will do us no harm, since we have not touched you, and since we have done nothing to you but good and have sent you away in peace. You are now the blessed of the Lord."*
>
> Genesis 26:29

That was a little hypocritical, wasn't it? The Philistines had done nothing but harass Isaac since the day he had arrived among them, stopping up his wells, claiming others of his wells for themselves, and even asking him to move away from them. But now they had laid down all of their pride because it was so obvious that he was *"the blessed of the Lord."*

Isaac's response to all of this is absolutely amazing:

> *So he made them a feast, and they ate and drank. Then they arose early in the morning and swore an oath with one another; and Isaac sent them away, and they departed from him in peace.* Genesis 26:30-31

Now, this is a lot for most people to stomach. "Didn't Isaac go too far?" I can hear some asking. But let me remind you again of the words of one of Jesus' most powerful messages:

When You Have Done the Right Thing

But I say to you, love your enemies, bless those who curse you, do good to those who hate you, and pray for those who spitefully use you and persecute you, that you may be sons of your Father in heaven; for He makes His sun rise on the evil and on the good, and sends rain on the just and on the unjust.

Matthew 5:44-45

The verbs *"love," "bless," "do,"* and *"pray,"* are not requests; they are in the imperative form, and thus, they are in the imperative form, and thus, they are commands. *"Love your enemies,"* Jesus said. *"Bless those who curse you," "do good to those who hate you,"* and *"pray for those who spitefully use you and persecute you."* That's true Christianity.

> *Isaac was sure that his Philistine neighbors hated him, but he decided to love them anyway.*

Isaac was sure that his Philistine neighbors hated him, but he decided to love them anyway. He was under no illusions. These were the same people who had stopped up his father's wells, had bickered with him over every well he dug or redug for himself, and had tried to lay claim to all that he had. And there could be no doubt that Abimelech was the same man who had asked him to leave. Still, he blessed them all. I wonder what you or I might have done under the same circumstances.

There is nothing to indicate that Isaac gloated over his victory or that he rubbed it in that his newfound friends had changed. He just prepared a party and treated them all well. Then, after the covenant had been cut, he sent them all away in peace. I find that to be an awesome example for all of us to follow.

Almost immediately, more blessing poured in for Isaac, the peacemaker:

It came to pass the same day that Isaac's servants came and told him about the well which they had dug, and said to him, "We have found water." Genesis 26:32

Isn't that amazing? On the very same day that he forgave the men who hated him and did good to them, good news came to him about his well. Not every well dug in that part of the world was productive, but the news this time was: *"We have found water."* When Isaac acted like a child of God and did the right thing by his enemies, water flowed to him the same day.

Do you have some wells that are not producing? Maybe God has held the waters back until you do the right thing by your enemies. Until you prove that you are mature enough to handle progress, there are some things that God will withhold from you. Having enemies is just part of the process, and until we learn to treat our enemies right, we're not ready for all that God has for us.

Again, we must not take it personally when people oppose us. They are not really opposing us, but opposing God. They don't hate us; they hate God. Jesus made this clear to His disciples:

Remember the word that I said unto you, The servant is not greater than his lord. If they have persecuted me, they will also persecute you; if they have kept my saying, they will keep yours also. But all these things will they do unto you for my name's sake, because they know not him that sent me.
John 15:20-21

Also know that God wants to use you to reach many of those who are currently your enemies. Expect people to begin noticing that water is flowing in your life and that nothing has stopped you from moving forward. Expect them to start coming to you for help, and prepare yourself to give it. People who have hurt you in the past will now respect you and want what you have. They will want God in their lives as they see Him in yours. If nothing else, people will recognize that they cannot beat you, and so they will join you.

When they come for your help, I pray that you are not in a retaliatory mood, and that you don't send them away empty handed. If you take that attitude, you just might lose all that you have gained to this point. The true test of whether or not you can handle the next level of progress and blessing that God has in store for you will be how you treat your enemies.

The minute Isaac blessed his enemies, made a covenant with them, and sent them away in peace, water started flowing in his newest well. No sooner had he done the right thing than his servants were coming with the good news. I am convinced that God is prepared to let water start flowing in your life too, and I encourage you to do the right thing.

God has a way of turning things around, and soon whatever was backward in your life will be turned forward. Whatever was going wrong will start going right. Where there was a shortage in the past, there will now be an overflow. When you do what is right and God sees that He can trust you and bless you, He will open up a floodgate in your life. Are you ready for it?

What is popular, easy, or desirable is not always what is right, but when you do right—even if it is unpopular, difficult, or not to your liking—water begins to flow. Every time you bless an enemy, you dig another well. Every time you pray for them, you dig another well. Every time you do good to them, you dig another well. And when the time is right, God will allow all your wells to spring forth with water.

He wants water to be flowing into every area of your life. So why not believe for it? Why not give the right thing a try? And when you have done the right thing, your current flow will turn into an overflow.

I would like to come into agreement with you that your life will turn around and that soon you will strike water. May the blessing of the Lord be so rich upon your life that the resulting flow will extend to many generations to come.

This story of Isaac's blessing ends in this way:

> *So he called it [the new well] Shebah [oath]. Therefore the name of the city is Beersheba [well of the oath] to this day.*
> Genesis 26:33

This is your time. Follow the necessary process, and you will make the desired progress. And in the doing of it, you will be *Surviving the Crisis.*

PART II

"WHEN I AM WEAK, THEN I AM STRONG"

CHAPTER 5

THE THORNS THAT AFFLICT US

And lest I should be exalted above measure by the abundance of the revelations, a thorn in the flesh was given to me, a messenger of Satan to buffet me, lest I be exalted above measure. Concerning this thing I pleaded with the Lord three times that it might depart from me. And He said to me, "My grace is sufficient for you, for My strength is made perfect in weakness." Therefore, most gladly I will rather boast in my infirmities, that the power of Christ may rest upon me. Therefore I take pleasure in infirmities, in reproaches, in needs, in persecutions, in distresses, for Christ's sake. For when I am weak, then I am strong. 2 Corinthians 12:7-10

The great apostle Paul had a problem, a crisis, if you will. His problem was so grievous that he prayed about it several times, asking God to take it away from him. Still, this thing did not leave him.

Whatever it was, Paul called it *"a thorn in the flesh"* and *"a messenger of Satan."* This shows clearly that it was not something desirable. It buffeted Paul, making him feel uncomfortable.

Interestingly enough, Paul began this passage by explaining why this thing had been permitted to torment him in the first place: *"lest I should be exalted above measure by the abundance of the revelations."* So there was a good reason for it.

Paul went on to describe what was happening to him with the

thorn, the messenger of Satan that buffeted him, and then he repeated again the purpose he saw for this happening: *"lest I be exalted above measure."* By repeating again this noble purpose for the suffering he was undergoing, Paul strengthened our understanding of the fact that thorns in the flesh exist, they are sent by God, and they serve a good purpose in our lives. That should allow many of us to relax and take more in stride some of the things that have, until now, been bothering our spirits.

> *Are you and I in any danger of being exalted today in the twenty-first century? Oh yes.*

Yes, Paul had a problem, but he had come to understand that there was a reason for it, and after praying about it several times, he came to the realization that this thing was actually for his benefit. Why should he try to get rid of it? It was uncomfortable, and he didn't like it, but it served a good purpose in his spiritual life. So he could bear it—by the grace of God.

Are you and I in any danger of being exalted today in the twenty-first century? Oh yes. We Christians call ourselves believers, and by that we mean that we believe in God, and we believe in His Word. Whatever our level of spiritual development, we seek to govern our lives by His dictates.

We say that we walk by faith and not by sight, and by that we mean that we are inspired and moved, not by what we can see, but by the revelation of His Word to us. Our faith is initially ignited and later expanded by what we hear coming from God through the preaching of His Word. Paul himself declared:

Faith cometh by hearing, and hearing by the word of God.
Romans 10:17, KJV

The Thorns that Afflict Us

Spiritually, ours is a most enlightened age. We have many means of hearing from God, most of us have heard from Him many times, and many of our plans have been shaped by what He has spoken to us—directly and through other men and women of God. In this way, we are a very peculiar people, very different from the average person of the world, and we don't behave anything like other people do. Those who don't know our God must see before they can believe, but we do just the opposite. We believe, and then we see.

Our every belief is anchored by our faith in God, and again, our faith in God is produced and watered by what we hear through the preaching of the Word of God. But even when we are constantly fed and watered, we sometimes develop a warped sense of understanding about what God is saying, and our much knowledge sometimes leads us to pride.

Sometimes in our walk with the Lord we find ourselves on a winning streak. There may be some small losses mixed in with our wins, but for the most part, we're on a roll. We are gaining revelation that is pushing us forward and upward. But this may be a dangerous point for us. The danger is that at some point we will begin to think of ourselves *"more highly than [we] ought"*:

> *For I say, through the grace given to me, to everyone who is among you, not to think of himself more highly than he ought to think, but to think soberly, as God has dealt to each one a measure of faith.*   Romans 12:3

Even the great apostle Paul was concerned that he might be *"exalted above measure."* And he believed that God had given him a *"thorn in the flesh"* precisely to prevent this danger. So thorns of this type are from God, and many of the things we have attributed to Satan were not his fault after all. God permitted them so that we would not become proud. We mistakenly give Satan far too much credit.

SURVIVING THE CRISIS

When God is doing so much for us and saying so much to us, we sometimes get to the place that we almost feel that we could fly, or, at the very least, walk on clouds. The richness and depth of the revelation given to us through His Word, as we frequent the House of the Lord, has a rather intoxicating effect, and we feel ourselves rising higher and higher. The danger is that we will not give God all the glory He deserves, but will become exalted through all of this.

God knows this, and He graciously sends our way some thorn or other (I believe that every one of us has one or more of them) to keep us on the ground and to keep us pressing forward.

Some of the thorns God sends our way are quite small, but even something small has the effect of keeping us struggling upward, so that we don't become too impressed with ourselves.

It seems that no matter how well things are going for us, no matter how productive and progressive we have become, no matter how much we are accomplishing, at least one thing will still exist to continue nagging at our spirits. We rebuke the devil, trying to get rid of it, and we pray earnestly in faith, asking the Lord to take it away, but, to our dismay, the thing persists.

The presence of such a thorn is troubling to us. In most other areas of our lives, we're winning. We have made many former enemies into footstools. God has moved obstacles and people out of our way, and areas of our lives that seemed irreparable have been fixed. Yes, the enemy has tried to step in and tear us down, but every time he has tried, the Lord has been there to stop him. He makes a way where there is no way and opens doors that have been previously shut in our faces. So, we know Him well as Deliverer.

Still, although we have sought Him for this one small area of life many times, victory seems illusive. The same thing keeps being thrown back in our faces time and time again, and it causes us to feel like a failure.

The Thorns that Afflict Us

"Oh God," we cry out, "why is it that I'm able to walk in victory in so many other areas of my life, and this one thing continues to nag at me? This thing is so small, and yet it seems to be rocking my world. You delivered me so quickly from many other things, but this thing just seems to hold on."

We don't mind pain that lasts for just a few days, but this pain never seems to go away. We have thought we could ride out the storm, but we never anticipated that this storm would go on for so long.

Some of us have little nagging issues that we've been working on for months and even years without seeing a breakthrough. We have fasted and prayed about it, sowed financial seeds dedicated to it, and still the thing continues to haunt us.

As time goes on, the pain of it becomes more and more unbearable. This tiny thing is now buffeting us so that we are being rocked from left to right and up and down. At times, we have thought we made some progress with it, but the moment we were sure we were at the point of total victory, the thing came back with even more intensity.

Many feel like they are all alone in this situation. Surely other Christians are not going through such a thing. But the apostle Paul did, and if he did, we can expect others to experience it too. Why would we expect to be better than him?

Paul was receiving many great revelations from God. After all, he became the author of a major part of the New Testament. Those sacred words came to him by revelation:

No prophecy of Scripture is of any private interpretation, for prophecy never came by the will of man, but holy men of God spoke as they were moved by the Holy Spirit.

2 Peter 1:20-21

The letters of Paul do not contain his personal opinions, but are filled with the abundant revelations he was receiving from God. Since a great part of our Christian doctrines rest upon the teachings of this man, we could not in any way minimize his wealth of revelation. His teachings on love, on grace, on sanctification, on justification, and on a host of other important subjects form the backbone of our understanding of the Christian way of life. Paul's writings teach us much about how a Christian should behave, and we owe him a great debt of gratitude. Thank God that he was open to the Holy Spirit to receive such an abundance of revelation. Next to Jesus, there is probably no individual of greater importance in the New Testament than Paul, and yet this great man suffered from a thorn in the flesh. That should speak to us all. This is just a part of the normal Christian life.

Paul also thought that such a thing should be removed from him. If God was doing so many great things for him, why couldn't He do this too? And Paul prayed to that end. In fact, he prayed about it three times, he tells us.

The first time Paul prayed, it seems that God didn't answer at all. The second time he prayed, God did not give him any assurance that He would remove the thorn. It was only the third time Paul prayed about it that he received an answer.

At last! This is what Paul had been waiting for for so long, but the answer he received that day was not the answer he had been wanting or expecting. Instead of hearing, "Of course, Paul, I will remove this thing," he heard the Lord say, *"My grace is sufficient for you, for My strength is made perfect in weakness."*

Again, this was not Paul's opinion. When he wrote this down, he was relaying to the Corinthian believers exactly what the Lord had said to him. God was urging him (and all others who would later hear this word) to understand how He works. He doesn't always answer our prayers by altering our circumstances or by removing our burdens. He could very easily place an anointing upon one of His servants to do that. Such an anointing is yoke-destroying and burden-removing. Isaiah said:

> *And it shall come to pass in that day, that his burden shall be taken away from off thy shoulder, and his yoke from off thy neck, and the yoke shall be destroyed because of the anointing.*   Isaiah 10:27, KJV

There is no question that God can do it, but does He want to do it? He knows what He is doing, and He doesn't always choose to lift every burden from us. Some of them are strategically placed there for a purpose, and if He removed them, He would be hindering our spiritual progress.

> *There is no question that God can do it, but does He want to do it?*

God doesn't always answer when we pray, because we often pray against what is best for us. Our tears cannot move Him to an action that would be counterproductive for His children. He knows best, and He must act in our best interests—whether we understand it or not.

God *does* hear our prayers and see our sacrifice in fasting. He *does* see our tears, and He knows exactly what we are suffering at the moment. But when we pray for something to be removed that He has put there Himself, or at the very least allowed to be put there, He *cannot* respond affirmatively. He is the sovereign God, and we must bow to His will, knowing that He always has our best interests at heart and that all things are working for our good.

SURVIVING THE CRISIS

Again, it was Paul who wrote to the Romans:

> *And we know that all things work together for good to those who love God, to those who are the called according to His purpose.* Romans 8:28

Let God be God, and let Him do things His own way. The thorns He sends our way are for our benefit. Accept them rather than struggle against them, thus *Surviving the Crisis.*

CHAPTER 6

THE GRACE THAT SUSTAINS US

And He said to me, "My grace is sufficient for you, for My strength is made perfect in weakness." Therefore, most gladly I will rather boast in my infirmities, that the power of Christ may rest upon me. Therefore I take pleasure in infirmities, in reproaches, in needs, in persecutions, in distresses, for Christ's sake. For when I am weak, then I am strong.

2 Corinthians 12:9-10

God doesn't always answer our prayers by fixing our situations, by delivering us from the current crisis, but rather He answers by giving us what we need to survive every crisis—His grace.

Grace—what is it? Grace has often been defined as the unmerited favor of God. It is God's way of giving us something that we need even when we have done nothing to deserve it. If we could earn grace, we would reduce it to mere legalism. Legalism is the requirement to live by a set of man-made rules in order to obtain righteousness, and where legalism abounds, grace is absent.

There is nothing that we can do to earn God's grace, and there is nothing that we can do to earn His righteousness, or holiness. Holiness, contrary to popular opinion, is not something that we can teach another person to do, and neither is righteousness. Righteousness comes to us when we have made a personal decision to walk with God, and the same is true of holiness. We become righteous through Him, not by anything that we do ourselves.

Just as grace cannot be earned, we also cannot position ourselves to receive it. This unmerited favor from God is a great mystery in that one day He just decides to do something for you, when you and He both know that you don't deserve it. Most of us can testify to the truth that, were it not for God's grace, we could not have come this far.

So how does grace work? Imagine that you have one son. One day you come home and find that your son has been brutally murdered. In rage, you go out looking for the killer, and with the help of the police, you find him. Now you have several choices: (1.) You could beat the living daylights out of the man and leave him half dead. That's what we call *vengeance,* and it is often the first thing we want to do. (2.) You could allow the courts to try and convict the man and possibly execute him if he is found guilty. That's what we call *justice.* But there is another alternative. (3.) You could forgive the man who killed your son, go to court and plead for his pardon, then, when the court frees him, take him into your home and make him your adopted son. That's what we call real *grace.*

Grace actually came about in just that way. God sent His only Son Jesus into the world to redeem the world. Jesus was convicted and then killed by the very people He was sent to redeem. Still, God accepted those who were responsible for the murder of His only Son into His family as His adopted sons and daughters. That's amazing grace, and it's "greater than all our sins," as the popular hymn states.

Paul had a dilemma, and God said that the answer to it was grace. Paul had taken this matter to the Lord in sincerity and sought Him about it three times. He knew that he was walking in righteousness and that he was hearing from God. His letter on righteousness would be used by believers as a guide for many centuries to come, and in it, he wrote of his own experience.

He knew that his relationship with God was solid, and He was confident in what God had been saying to him and doing through him. He was sure that all things were working together for his good, because he loved God and was called according to His purpose. Still, he was desperate for an answer to his problem.

Paul could not have agreed more with what Peter wrote to the churches:

> *Therefore humble yourselves under the mighty hand of God, that He may exalt you in due time, casting all your care upon Him, for He cares for you.* 1 Peter 5:6-7

Paul was casting his cares upon the Lord now with all that was within him, but he was not getting the answer he so desired. What was up with God?

When God finally answered, Paul must have been very surprised with what He said, for as we have seen, the Lord's response was not at all what was expected. God had allowed this *"thorn in the flesh,"* this *"messenger of Satan"* to buffet Paul for a reason,

> *God accepted those who were responsible for the murder of His only Son into His family as His adopted sons and daughters.*

and therefore it would *not* be removed. Instead, he would be given grace to bear it.

This had to be surprising to Paul because he was saved, he loved the Lord, he was walking in obedience and doing everything he believed God was asking him to do. God was using him to change individuals, communities, and whole nations, and now why couldn't he get victory over something so small in his own personal life?

That didn't seem to make sense. Paul knew God to be loving

and compassionate and all-powerful, and a God who answered the most simple prayer of His people. And yet that same God was saying no to this earnest prayer of the apostle. How could this be happening?

But, as much as He loved Paul, God *could not* remove this thorn. It had a good purpose, and it was necessary to the well-being of the apostle. Paul was receiving an abundance of revelation, so he needed something to keep his feet on the ground. If the thorn was removed prematurely, Paul might never reach his full potential.

Pride is a killer, and when we get puffed up (even because God is doing great things for us), we endanger our futures. If God places something in our lives that keeps us humble before Him, that thing—whatever it is—is worth everything to us. Why would God remove it?

There are some prayers that God always answers, and there are some things that He will always give you when you ask for them, but this is an exception. He will not give you something that is harmful to you, and He will not remove something from your life that is placed there for a useful purpose. If your prayer is, as it should be, that He will not allow your flesh to destroy your future, then the thorns He is sending your way are helping you to find the answer.

Sometimes God has to let a believer fall so that he will realize that he can't make it without the Lord's help. When this happens, it puts us all on notice that we cannot afford to take our God for granted. Just because a person is saved, just because a person hears from God, just because a person is experiencing great miracles or receiving wonderful revelation is no guarantee that they will not be overcome. The greatest man or woman of God can fall, and we must all guard ourselves against this terrible end.

Some thorns are worse than others, but all of us have a thorn in the flesh of some kind or other. We are able to do good deeds and to help others be set free, and yet we struggle with some nagging issue of our own. This thing—whatever it happens to be—is placed there in love by God Himself, and no amount of prayer will remove it. You must find the answer Paul found and get God's grace to overcome.

God doesn't want us to hurt ourselves. He doesn't want us to be spiritually spoiled. He doesn't want us to become exalted in our own eyes. So He sends something our way that continually reminds us: "You're not all that great!"

Paul was definitely a man of prayer, and he knew what it was to commune with God. He knew how to focus his prayers on specific issues, and he did it in this case ... three times. Still, nothing happened.

I understand why Paul was so persistent with this prayer. After all, how could he advise others when he had a problem of his own? Wouldn't they consider that hypocritical? God was speaking to him what to write to many churches, but how could he do that if he could not be totally free himself? So he asked God and he continued to ask God for deliverance from his own nagging thorn. But God's answer was *"grace."*

Grace? Paul hadn't asked for grace. He had asked for deliverance from something that was tormenting and troubling him. He didn't like it. It didn't seem compatible and consistent with his testimony, and he wanted to be rid of it. Surely nothing good could come of it. God loved him and wanted him free. So why could he not be free?

God doesn't always gives us what we want; He gives us what we need. That was the secret of Paul's answer. We often ask God for things that we want desperately, but they're not always good for us. And God knows that. His promise is clear:

SURVIVING THE CRISIS

And my God shall supply all your NEED according to His riches in glory by Christ Jesus. Philippians 4:19

He *"shall supply,"* but not absolutely everything you ask Him for. He *"shall supply ALL YOUR NEED."* He is rich, and He can easily give you everything you need, but He knows better than you what that is.

It is rather shocking to think that not all of Paul's prayers were answered, but that's the truth of it. He asked for deliverance from his thorn, for that's what he wanted. God, instead, gave him something far greater, something he needed—His grace.

> *God refused to remove the thorn that was tormenting Paul, and He refused to change his situation.*

God refused to remove the thorn that was tormenting Paul, and He refused to change his situation. He is not a handyman on call to us to do this and that, or whatever repair work we require. We sometimes forget that He is the Lord, and we are His servants. He will not necessarily do what you want Him to do in the moment you want Him to do it and in the way you want Him to do it. But if not, He'll give you something better.

"God, fix it," is one of the most common prayers prayed these days, and sometimes He does. But sometimes He chooses not to. Trust Him that He knows what's best for your life in every given situation.

God is still in control, and He is still the all-sufficient One, but He reserves the right to use His power in a way that pleases Him and works toward His desired ends. He may not handle a given situation in the way you want Him to, but if that happens, it will be because He has a better plan. His ways are clearly not our ways:

The Grace that Sustains Us

"For My thoughts are not your thoughts,
Nor are your ways My ways," says the LORD.
"For as the heavens are higher than the earth,
So are My ways higher than your ways,
And My thoughts than your thoughts."   Isaiah 55:8-9

We must trust God. If He doesn't fix something it means that He will fix us to face that thing. Some people are so stubborn that they refuse to accept this. "This thing *will* go," they insist. Well, are you more powerful than the apostle Paul? God will deliver you, but He'll do it in His own way. If He doesn't do what you ask Him to do, then expect Him to do *"exceedingly abundantly above all that we ask or think"* (Ephesians 3:20), and know that His ways are always best.

It is very important that each of us makes a commitment to God that whether He fixes our particular situation or not, we will continue to serve Him. He is mighty, and He is loving, and if He is not answering me, it must mean that He has something better in mind. Trust His goodness, and never become angry that your prayers are not answered. Rather, try to bring your prayers more in line with God's overall will for your life.

God says to you today what He said to Paul in the first century: *"My grace is sufficient for you."* His grace is all over your life, and that's all you need.

After Paul received that unexpected answer from God, he realized that he should *"boast"* in his *"infirmities"* and *"take pleasure"* in such things as *"reproaches," "needs," "persecutions,"* and *"distresses."* None of those sound like much fun to me, but Paul came to realize that these things were his servants, and they were helping him be the best man he could be for God. Rather than struggle with them, he must learn to deal with them through God's grace.

Paul spoke of praying only three times about this matter, so it seems that once he received the revelation of God's grace, he no longer had to ask for God's help with it. God's grace *was* sufficient.

I'm sure that Paul must have been asking God for more power, and now, because of the thorn that was allowed to buffet him, he had the power he sought. If you got rid of all the things that trouble you, you just might lose your power with God. But if you stay right there, and let the anointing of grace help you weather the storm, you'll become more powerful every day.

Every now and again, when you pray and ask God to do something for you, He will be silent, or He will decline to help you. This will not mean that you are alienated from Him or that you are not living right. It will just mean that He is doing something special in your life. When it happens, pray as Jesus did:

> *"Father, if it is Your will ... ; nevertheless not My will, but Yours, be done."*   Luke 22:42

If God has not answered your prayer for deliverance, it will be because He is leaving you in the battle long enough to learn something new. Soon, you will have enough grace, not only to pull yourself through, but also to help pull others through.

And never complain in your weakness and pain. That's a waste of time. Start bragging about the grace of God. One of our old favorite hymns says it this way:

> *I have found His grace is all complete,*
> *He supplieth every need,*
> *While I sit and learn at Jesus' feet,*
> *I am free, yes, free indeed.*

And the chorus speaks of "joy unspeakable and full of glory," and concludes with the truth: "Oh, the half has never yet been told."

The Grace that Sustains Us

Though Satan may buffet, though trials may come, I'm free. I don't care that a messenger of Satan might rise up against me. It will become my servant. By the grace of God, I'm free. I'm *Surviving the Crisis.*

CHAPTER 7

"I AM WHAT I AM
BY THE GRACE OF GOD"

But by the grace of God I am what I am, and His grace toward me was not in vain; but I labored more abundantly than they all, yet not I, but the grace of God which was with me.   1 Corinthians 15:10

Oddly enough, one of the greatest struggles many believers seem to be having these days, a crisis, if you please, is the inability to admit the truth about themselves. This is serious because we need real people in God's army in this twenty-first century. Many act as if they were always saved, as if they have never done a single thing wrong, and we know that this cannot be true. The psalmist declared:

> *Behold, I was brought forth in iniquity,*
> *And in sin my mother conceived me.*   Psalm 51:5

None of us can say that our lives have been sinless, and it's time that we stop putting on a holy front and living as hypocrites. We have been redeemed, and that means that we had something to be redeemed *from*. Our Savior loosed us from the shackles of sin, and there are still people alive who know what we were before He did that. So stop pretending that you have always lived a perfect life. Those of us who are members of the Body of Christ are so only by the grace and mercy of God—no other way.

Paul had many spiritual accomplishments. For instance, God used him to establish many of the early churches and to write to them, relaying the divine message, and, in this way establishing for all generations to come the Word of God. Still, Paul needed grace and was nothing without it. He was what he was only because of the grace of God, so what more can *you* expect?

> When you truly depend on God's grace, that grace will not be in vain in your life.

Paul went a step further, stating that the grace of God that had been extended to him had not been in vain. Because he knew that he was what he was only by God's grace, he used that grace to benefit God's Kingdom. He even felt the necessity to *"labor more abundantly"* than others. The fact that it took more than he had to make him what he was inspired him to work harder.

The great apostle Paul hadn't been able to save himself; it was only the grace of God that changed him. Grace doesn't come from working in the church, and when we act as though we are self-made people, we place a stain on the Body of Christ. This type of hypocrisy drives many away from the church. People everywhere hate liars, deceivers, and hypocrites.

Paul was not afraid to declare that he had been nothing in himself and that only the grace of God had made him what he now was. He *had* been religious, but he had persecuted the true believers. Now, here he was preaching the very Gospel he had formerly persecuted. What was the reason for this dramatic transformation? It was grace, and nothing but grace.

Don't be afraid of your past history. Unless you remember who you were before, you can't possibly appreciate who you are now. When you see the original product as it was, and then you realize that God thought enough of you in that condition to pick you up from the trash heap, brush you off, cleanse you thoroughly, and then give you respectability, it causes you to appreciate God and the work He has done in you.

You can't take the credit for what you are now. There's no way you could have come this far. It wasn't your education that made you what you are today; only grace could do that.

And when you truly depend on God's grace, that grace will not be in vain in your life. Make up your mind that because God gave you another chance, manifested His grace in you, and made you somebody, you will now work harder for Him.

Never allow yourself to get puffed up, arrogant, or selfish. You are who you are only by God's grace, so show Him how much you appreciate what He has done for you by your attitude and by your works. People who have an appreciation for the grace of God cannot remain inactive in the church for long. They cannot live their lives without trying to make everything they do a testimony to others. They never look down on others, for they know where they have come from themselves, and they know that they would be nothing without God's grace. When we see other people in terrible messes, it only reminds us of the mess God got us out of through His grace. When we see people down, we think of the opportunity such people have to get up, just as we got up after we were down.

Grace frees us from several things. First, it frees us from ourselves. Some people live in a penitentiary they have constructed for themselves, and they are captives to their past. They live every day hoping against hope that no one will find out who they are, or at least who they were. But the easiest way to handle the past is to talk about it openly and willingly. Why should you be afraid to tell people where you came from?

Don't risk creating for yourself a prison of your past life. That would be a terrible way to live, and those who are in such a prison will never make an impact upon others.

Grace not only frees us from ourselves, but it also frees us from others and from the tyranny of their expectations, opinions, and demands. Far too many Christians are enslaved in this regard today. The best way to deal with this problem is just to live your life to please the One who gave you grace, and let everyone else come along for the ride if they want to. Let them know up front that they can get off at any time. It's their choice. But you simply cannot live your life to please everybody and his neighbor. It takes too much effort, and it's not worth it.

You will very rarely be able to please everyone, so stop trying. Love people, and treat them respectfully, and be at peace with everyone you possibly can, as Paul taught:

> *If it is possible, as much as depends on you, live peaceably with* > *all men.* Romans 12:18

But stop trying to please everyone and to make everyone like you. If the truth were to be known, there are probably some people in this world who are anointed to hate you. You could be kind to them every day, take them to lunch once a week, and buy them a gift every time you travel, but that would not change the way they feel about you one bit. They would eat your lunches and enjoy them, and they would receive your gifts and appreciate them, but they still wouldn't change their way of thinking about you as a person. Despite everything you do for them, they will continue to dislike you, lie about you, and try to defame your character.

Don't lose any sleep over people who act like this. Keep dishing out grace to them, and let God do the rest. You can't change them, so stop trying. But whatever you do, don't struggle to change *your* personality to suite the tastes of others. You will never fit into someone else's mold. Allow God's grace to make you who you are—and be happy with that.

Determine that you are who you are by the grace of God, and if others are not happy with that, it's their problem, not yours. As God's grace shapes you more and more, you will be even more different, and consequently, more at odds with those who are of this world. If you have to lose friends and acquaintances to do the will of God, then so be it. Losing someone's friendship is never easy, but God will see to it that His all-sufficient grace is there to keep you through the experience.

God's grace frees us from ourselves and from the opinions of others, and it also frees us from any unforgiveness that might still be found in our hearts. We can make such wonderful strides in this area that we will be able to forgive those who have not even apologized and asked for our forgiveness. And that does take grace.

When this kind of grace is at work in your life, you can know that people have done things to hurt you, and yet you can be kind to them. When this happens, you'll know for sure that grace is working in your life. But if you have enjoyed the unmerited favor of God in your own life, the least you can do is extend that same grace to others.

I am aware that forgiveness is one of the most difficult things you might be called upon to do, but if grace could save you and, in the process, forgive you for all of the wrongs you committed in the past, then grace can help you to forgive others as well. I'm aware that many people find it difficult to forgive even when a person apologizes to them and asks forgiveness. And how much more difficult the process becomes when there is seemingly no remorse on the part of others, and certainly no apology! But that shouldn't matter. Grace makes complete forgiveness not only doable, but also easy. God's grace is sufficient, and it is sufficient to free you from every yoke of unforgiveness.

Unforgiveness is still one of the greatest problems we are facing in the church today. And why is that? If God has forgiven us for so much, why can't we, in turn, forgive others for so little? How do Christians expect to get into heaven with hearts filled with hatred for others? There is no such thing as an anointed hatred, or an anointed grudge, and unforgiveness is never anointed. May the grace of God free us from such bondages to the past.

Make up your mind today that you will forgive others. This is important to your own spiritual well-being in more ways than one. Jesus taught us to pray:

> *Forgive us our debts,*
> *As we forgive our debtors.*   Matthew 6:12

He went on to say:

> *For if you forgive men their trespasses, your heavenly Father*
> *will also forgive you. But if you do not forgive men their tres-*
> *passes, neither will your Father forgive your trespasses.*
> Matthew 6:14-15

There can be no doubt that Jesus forged an unbreakable link between our willingness to forgive others and His willingness to continue forgiving us. When people have said things to us and about us that they should not have said and done things to us that they should not have done, we sometimes hope that God will keep them out of view. If we see them, we're not sure just how we might react. After all, there is only so much a person can take. But grace is sufficient for all our hurts and wrongs. Some of us would rather that

God hold onto His grace long enough to allow us to give the person in question what he deserves, but that's definitely not a Christian attitude.

I'm writing from experience. I've known people I didn't feel like forgiving. After what they had done, I actually wanted God to kill them. But then, when I had time to think about it, I realized that there were times in the past when God could have killed me too, and I'm still here. I am what I am because of the grace of God, and because God has shown me so much grace, I must show grace to others. Yes, it's hard, but God's grace is sufficient.

> *There can be no doubt that Jesus forged an unbreakable link between our willingness to forgive others and His willingness to continue forgiving us.*

Many Christians, long after they have been forgiven for the deeds of their past, are still suffering under what I have some to call a "tyranny of ought." They are constantly being heard to say, "I ought to have done this" or "I ought to have done that." They are saved, they pray and read God's Word, and they witness and do many other good works, but the more they do, the less they seem to enjoy it. Some actually become workaholics for God, trying to forget the past, and without grace, you can work yourself to death and have no reward to show for it.

Working for God is good, and we should do more of it, but working endlessly without grace is a drudgery that will leave any man or woman exhausted. Begin to recognize the grace of God at work in your life, and conduct yourself before others as one who is what he is only by the grace of God. If you rely on your anointing to get you where you need to go—or your gift or your knowledge—you are surely on your way to death and destruction. You and I are nothing without the grace of God, and without His grace at work in us, we will not be *Surviving the Crisis*.

CHAPTER 8

GOD'S GIFTS TO YOU

Seeing that we have a great High Priest who has passed through the heavens, Jesus the son of God, let us hold fast our confession. For we do not have a High Priest who cannot sympathize with our weaknesses, but was in all points tempted as we are, yet without sin. Let us therefore come boldly before the THRONE OF GRACE, that we might obtain MERCY AND GRACE to help in a time of need. Hebrews 4:14-16

At God's throne, here called *"the throne of grace,"* we can obtain two gifts, mercy and grace, to help us in our time of need, or crisis. Mercy is a topic that more of us seem to understand. "Lord, have mercy on me" is a very common cry among believers. But these two elements, mercy and grace, are not synonymous. Mercy does something for us, but grace causes us to do something for God.

It's just human nature to cry out to God when we are in trouble, to want Him to do something for us, but grace demands that we do something for Him and for others. Mercy blesses us, but grace stretches us. Mercy delivers us, but grace challenges us. Mercy restores us, but it takes grace to preserve us. Mercy meets us at the door, but grace takes us inside.

When the prodigal son returned home to his father, the father ran to meet him. That's mercy. But before the son could get back into his father's house, he had to recognize grace at work and come to the conclusion that he would rather be a hired servant in his father's house than remain a son living in a pig pen.

Mercy will spare you, but grace seals you until the day of redemption. Goodness and mercy will follow you, but it's grace that will guide you.

Paul admonishes us that when we approach the throne of God, we are there to obtain mercy and find grace to help in the time of need. He was speaking from experience. A man of sterling reputation, he nevertheless had said that he was what he was only because of God's grace. In another of his letters to the churches, this one to the Corinthian believers, Paul wrote (as we have seen in previous chapters):

> *And lest I should be exalted above measure by the abundance of the revelations, a thorn in the flesh was given to me, a messenger of Satan to buffet me, lest I be exalted above measure. Concerning this thing I pleaded with the Lord three times that it might depart from me. And He said to me, "My grace is sufficient for you, for My strength is made perfect in weakness." Therefore, most gladly I will rather boast in my infirmities, that the power of Christ may rest upon me. Therefore I take pleasure in infirmities, in reproaches, in needs, in persecutions, in distresses, for Christ's sake. For when I am weak, then I am strong.* 2 Corinthians 12:7-10

Amazingly, Paul learned to actually *"take pleasure"* in such unpleasant things as *"infirmities," "reproaches," "needs," "persecutions,"* and *"distresses,"* and he did it *"for Christ's sake."* He came to realize that all of this was for his benefit, and grace enabled him to remain at peace through it all. He ended this passage with an amazing statement: *"For when I am weak, then I am strong."* That doesn't seem to make sense, does it? Paul meant that it was in his weakness that God's grace could be manifested, and therefore in his weakness, he could be strong. His strength was not a strength of the flesh, but a strength of the Spirit.

Our adversaries are often shocked when they confront us that we don't react as they expect us to. When we are attacked, it would be only normal for our flesh to react, but when we realize that we are weak in the flesh and depend on God's mercy, then we're suddenly strong and can stand against any enemy.

As we saw in Chapter 5, because of an abundance of revelations, a messenger of Satan was sent to Paul to buffet him lest he be exalted above measure. This thorn in the flesh was a gift from God, and one of the reasons God permits such a thorn in our lives is so that in the midst of the buffeting, we can know that all is well with our souls.

> *Our adversaries are often shocked when they confront us that we don't react as they expect us to.*

Paul prayed three times that his thorn would be removed from him, but God's answer was no. Instead, He said, He was giving Paul grace to overcome his trial, and that grace, He added, was sufficient for his every need. When Satan comes against us, we don't have to react badly, as he hopes we will. God has given us a gift that will enable us to survive and thrive in the midst of our trials.

Grace plays a very serious role in our salvation:

> *And when he [Paul] was disposed to pass into Achaia, the brethren wrote, exhorting the disciples to receive him: who, when he was come, helped them much which had believed through grace.*
>
> Acts 18:27

We are saved by faith, but our salvation comes *"through grace."*

SURVIVING THE CRISIS

For by grace you have been saved through faith, and that not of yourselves; it is the gift of God.   Ephesians 2:8

Here it is stated even more powerfully. We are saved *"by grace,"* and *"it is the gift of God."* In Paul's case, the thorn in the flesh was a gift, and the grace to overcome it was also a gift. God loved him so much that He sent him two wonderful gifts. One of these gifts was to help Paul, and the other gift was to humble Paul. The humbling was necessary because of the powerful way God had been dealing with Paul, the things He had been doing in his life, and the great future He had planned for him. The thorn gift kept his feet on the ground.

Both gifts had their purpose and their place, and both were for Paul's good. He couldn't experience the fullness of God's power without a thorn to help him stay humble. It kept him balanced. But what specifically are we talking about when we refer to a *"thorn in the flesh"*? Let us consider several common scenarios.

In some cases, a man will have a nice home to live in, a modern vehicle to drive, good clothes to wear, and some money in his pocket. It might seem that he has everything he could ever want. But look closely, and you might find that his wife is a trying person. She may even be unfaithful to him. His children are doing well in school, and if his wife could just be faithful and stop making a fool of him, he feels that he could gain the respect in the community and church he so richly deserves. That's his particular thorn.

A thorn is never something that you can remove on your own. If you could, it would not be a true thorn. You can never find a suitable solution for yourself. The grace of God, however, can equip you to ride out the accompanying storm.

Consider another possible scenario. A lady has a husband who is very faithful and caring. He helps her with the cooking and cleaning and even with the washing and ironing. He picks her and the children up when they need him to. He sounds like a dream come true, but the problem is that he's always broke. The family has no more today than they did years ago. If he had anything, he would share it with his wife and children, but he has nothing. He can't seem to make any financial progress, and this is her thorn in the flesh. She can be glad about the fact that he does not keep sweethearts, but she would like to enjoy the bare essentials of life.

On the other hand, some husbands are very good providers. Their problem is that they never do any maintenance at home. The toilet backs up frequently, the garage door won't close properly, and rats overrun their home. We should never judge other people, because we have no idea what they are having to bear in their personal lives.

And be careful what you think of others for another reason: Your turn is coming, for as sure as the sun rises, you will also experience some thorn in the flesh at some point. Rather than criticize others, we members of the Body of Christ should band together and let the strong bear the infirmities of the weak:

> *We then that are strong ought to bear the infirmities of the weak, and not to please ourselves.* Romans 15:1, KJV

Each of us receives a special gift from God called *"a thorn in the flesh,"* and that gift—as misunderstood and unwanted as it might be—has a good purpose in our lives. God would never have called a thorn a gift if it was not designed to bless us. But until the thorn in the flesh matures to the place that it can bless us, He gives us another gift—this one called grace. This gift of grace is never given to eliminate the thorn, but rather, to help us persevere until the thorn can fulfil its assignment.

For Paul, the thorn in his flesh clearly served a good purpose in his life, and this brought to him the revelation of the overcoming grace of God that would prove sufficient in the midst of his weaknesses. Often difficulties have to come to our lives so that we can experience a deeper revelation of the things of God, and sometimes this process is painful. Don't think for a moment that God will just allow you to plunge into His deepest secrets before you have proven to Him that you can persevere under severe scrutiny. So, you receive two balancing gifts. One of them pains you, and the other preserves you.

The worst thing a believer can do when he is in pain is to turn to sin. Some have decided that sin is a remedy for pain, and when they're feeling pain, they therefore submit to sin. In doing so, they accept Satan's lie that sin always brings pleasure, and they hope, in this way, to exchange pain for pleasure.

> *The worst thing a believer can do when he is in pain is to turn to sin.*

The problem with exchanging pain for pleasure is that the pleasure is only temporary, and once the pleasure has worn off, you realize that the pain has never really left you. If you will cling to the gift of grace in the midst of your trial and pain, the grace of God will enable you to move beyond pain. God's grace *is* sufficient, and it is sufficient for you in every situation.

The same God who walked with Adam in the cool of the day will abide with you in the heat of your trials, and His grace will be sufficient for you. The same God who called Abraham, blessed Jacob, and kept Isaac will stand by you in your intense moments of dilemma. The same God who met Moses at the burning bush and told him he would have to remove his shoes because the ground he was walking on was holy will also cause you to cast off your heavy bands and lift up your holy hands. You will do it with joy because you have come to understand that God's amazing grace is equal to the task you are currently dealing with in your life.

You have not been left alone to fend for yourself; you can't handle your thorn without God's help. That's why you need to realize that you are who you are because of the grace of God. When you have been delivered from anything, you must learn to thank the Lord properly. Your rejoicing makes room for your next miracle of deliverance.

I give God praise for making me who I am by His grace, and I pray that my open thanks given to Him in this way will inspire someone else to seek Him for their own deliverance. Praising God properly is a habit that more of us need to develop. It's a healthy attitude. We must be grateful to God for bringing us out of things we could not bring ourselves out of. We came out because His grace was sufficient for us.

God is righteous in His rule, and famous in His fullness. He's precious in His peace, judicious in His justice, bounteous in His blessing, constant in His care, definite in His defense, diligent in His devotion, absolute in His affection, beneficial in His benevolence, and matchless in His mercy. But most of all, our God is generous in His grace. His grace is sufficient for you, and will enable you to continuing *Surviving the Crisis.*

CHAPTER 9

UTILIZING THE SERVICES OF OUR GREAT HIGH PRIEST

Seeing then that we have a great High Priest who has passed through the heavens, Jesus the Son of God, let us hold fast our confession. For we do not have a High Priest who cannot sympathize with our weaknesses, but was in all points tempted as we are, yet without sin. Let us therefore come boldly to the throne of grace that we may obtain mercy and find grace to help in time of need.   Hebrews 4:14-16

And lest I should be exalted above measure by the abundance of revelations, a thorn in the flesh was given to me, a messenger of Satan to buffet me, lest I be exalted above measure. Concerning this thing I pleaded with the Lord three times that it might depart from me. And He said to me, "My grace is sufficient for you, for My strength is made perfect in weakness." ...
Therefore I take pleasure in infirmities, in reproaches, in needs, in persecutions, in distresses, for Christ sake. For when I am weak, then I am strong.   2 Corinthians 12:7-10

Nothing ever catches God by surprise, our crises included. He is the Sovereign God, and Jesus, our Lord, who is also our Great High Priest, is real and alive. Our testimonies must reflect these truths.

Let us be bearers of the fact that God always has the last word in everything, and His word is very different from our own. And, as we have seen, His ways are also not at all like our ways.

As believers in Christ, we know that we love Him, we know that He has called us and chosen us, and we know that we are serving Him. Still, things happen in our lives for which we have absolutely no explanation. We have to say that, since God is in control of all things, He has permitted these things to happen. How else could they happen?

> *As saved as we are and as righteous as we try to be, there are still things about us that don't seem to make sense.*

But why *do* they happen? As saved as we are and as righteous as we try to be, there are still things about us that don't seem to make sense.

We know that we feel God's presence with us, and we know that He is in us. The amazing thing to most of us is that He doesn't seem to be shocked by what is happening to us at the moment. That is sometimes very perplexing. We would have to say like Paul:

> *I have been crucified with Christ; it is no longer I who live, but Christ lives in me; and the life which I now live in the flesh I live by faith in the Son of God, who loved me and gave Himself for me.* Galatians 2:20

I have always found joy in the fact that Christ is living in me, and when things happen in my life that I can't understand, I console myself with this fact. And if He is not shocked and scandalized by what is happening to me, then I shouldn't be either. Nothing takes Him by surprise.

Our Great High Priest

Our Lord understands what I may not yet understand, precisely because His ways are not my ways, and the way He thinks is very different from the way I think. His living inside of me makes up for my insufficiencies and inadequacies. Thus, I can say with the apostle Paul that even though I am weak, I'm really strong. My flesh is weak, but I have Someone strong living inside of me, and that makes me strong too.

When I'm weak, this Person who is living inside of me manifests His grace—His unmerited favor. Thus, even in my weaknesses, God's strength is manifested. In fact, it is in the midst of our weaknesses, our human frailties, that we can best see the grace of God at work.

It is always a wonder to see how people of faith are able to ride through some insurmountable circumstance and are left standing, when others have been wiped out by the very same circumstance. This causes many to marvel. Still, the process of pressing through all that torments us is not always an easy one.

Because God doesn't think like we think, He often deals with us in ways that we are not expecting. He allows circumstances to come to us that seemingly leave us no choices. We are left wondering just what is happening to us. But we just *think* that we have no choices.

Because we are not all-knowing, as God is, our choices seem limited, but only because our thinking is limited, and our sight is limited. But there is Someone living inside of me who can see what I can't see and who can know what I can't know. He can take me where I can not otherwise go, He can bring things to my remembrance that I would have ordinarily forgotten, and He can cause me to receive revelation that is beyond the scope of my earthly concepts.

The secret then, of my successful Christian life, is for me to step back and push the great High Priest forward, thus tipping the balance in my life for good. If we can have more of Him and less of us, we can be consistently victorious.

Those who insist on pushing themselves forward are limiting themselves to what they can see and what they can do. If we push forward our great High Priest, He can cover our weaknesses and put to work His strength, cover our inabilities and let appear His ability, cover what we cannot handle and, by His grace, make something useful of our lives. His life in us can cause us to have peace in the midst of every storm.

In my opinion, it was Paul who wrote the book of Hebrews, and this writing helps us because it reminds us of the power of our great High Priest. The fact that He has *"passed through the heavens,"* enables us to *"hold fast to our confession."* But what exactly does that mean? I am convinced that it means that Jesus literally passed though everything that you and I will ever have to go through. Therefore, in the midst of whatever dilemma we happen to be in at the moment, we must never let go of our confession.

In this life, our faith will always be challenged. Things come to us that are designed by Satan to send our faith into an early retirement. If we pay attention only to what we can see, we may end up telling our faith to back off because it's not worth it. But, since we have a High Priest who has already passed through what we're currently passing through (and also what we are yet to pass through), we can be victorious through Him. What a privilege to be connected to such a High Priest!

Paul went on to emphasize the fact that our High Priest is not like some earthly priests. He can sympathize with what we are feeling: *"We do not have a High Priest who cannot sympathize with our weaknesses."* The King James Version renders the same passage in this way: *"We have not an high priest which cannot be touched with the feeling of our infirmities."* This word *infirmities* refers to our inabilities. We have a High Priest who can sympathize and empathize with us. He can feel what we feel.

In order to accomplish this, our High Priest gave up much. He laid down His kingly crown, stepped down from His throne, and came into this sinful and unfriendly world. Here, He allowed Himself to be wrapped in flesh and to be born as a common child.

After a very short life here on earth, our High Priest was condemned to death by evil men and crucified. On a cruel Roman cross, He suffered, bled, and died for us. Then, the worst torment came. He actually took our place in hell. But let the record show that He overcame it all, coming back to this world with power and authority to be seen of men in complete victory.

So, there is nothing in this world that any of us could ever face that our Great High Priest (to whom we are so closely connected) has not already experienced and cannot understand. Complaining about what we have to go through in life, therefore, is an exercise in futility. And worse, every time we complain, we glorify the devil. Since we have a High Priest who can be touched by the feeling of our infirmities, we must be slow to complain. Instead of complaining, let us do what the writer to the Hebrews recommended: *"Let us therefore come boldly to the throne of grace that we may obtain mercy and find grace to help in time of need."*

Coming boldly does not necessarily mean loudly or with an attitude. It simply means that we come in confidence. So, let us come in confidence to the throne of grace to obtain grace and mercy when we are in trouble. And the more we do this, the greater will be our confidence.

If we fail to go to the throne of grace when we are *not* in trouble, then it becomes difficult to build up the confidence we need to go there in our time of need. We must make a practice of going there when all is well. Make a habit of calling on God regularly, and when you desperately need Him, you'll have the confidence to call upon His name.

When we are not in need, we can go to God just to give thanks and worship Him. Make it a habit, and when you begin to call on

His name, have nothing special in mind to ask. Just be there to enjoy the fellowship of His presence. Then, when you *do* need Him, He will always be near.

You can be assured that He feels your pain, He knows what you are dealing with, and He is not shocked by what you are experiencing. His hands are outstretched to you, and He is saying, "My child, bring it to Me. I can handle it, because I've been there." So don't waste time complaining. Use your time to come boldly before His throne.

Be careful not to get a wrong picture of God in your mind. Some see Him as an obscure being sitting up high on a throne somewhere just waiting for them to sin so that He can punish them. No, our God is very different from that picture. He is ever beckoning to His children, showing us all that His throne room is open to us, and inviting us all to run to Him with our heartaches and cares. "Come," He says, "with all that is weighing you down. I can deal with it."

The primary responsibility of our High Priest is not to sit in judgment over us. There is a future time reserved for what we call The Judgment. But in the meantime, our High Priest sits as an Advocate at the hand of our Father to represent us and plead our cause before God. All we need to do is come to Him, and He knows how to handle our case.

Because of this, it is foolish to try to deal with the issues that hurt us by ourselves, that is without God's help. If a High Priest and Advocate has been provided for us, why not utilize His services?

To many people today, God is just some financier we go to when we are in need of a house or a car. But He is so much more than that. He can take care of all the things we can't handle ourselves. He has solutions for situations that are beyond our control. For instance, He can heal sicknesses for which no cure yet exists. He *is* our Provider, but He is much more. Isaiah declared:

Our Great High Priest

His name will be called
Wonderful, Counselor, Mighty God,
Everlasting Father, Prince of Peace.   Isaiah 9:6

Why would I not call on Him then? He is mighty to deliver. And, as our great High Priest, He is always available in our time of need.

Needs differ from one person to another, and even the needs of a given individual change. Things that I asked the Lord for ten years ago are no longer on my prayer list today. For instance, if God has provided us a house, we no longer need to ask Him for one. He has already proven Himself faithful in that area. If we have a car, and it's working, we would not want to exhaust our prayer time asking God for a new one some time in the future. If He provided one, He will provide another—when the need arises.

> *Our faith must be fixed, or focused, on areas of need.*

Our faith must be fixed, or focused, on areas of need. If our own concept of what is needed in our lives is lacking, as is often the case, we must ask the Lord to reveal to us what our most important needs are, so that we can refocus our prayers on those things. All of us can pray that our love for God be lifted to a greater level, that we can avoid hating people around us, and that we can be honest and true in all of our daily interactions. Then there are our very specific prayers, and we have many things to inquire of God about.

Go to Him for everything. Never go to a divorce court before first spending much time before the throne of grace seeking help and direction for your marriage. Don't make any major decision in your life before going in confidence to the throne of grace. Because of the seriousness of our times, it would not be wise for our young people to go out on a date without first going to the throne room and asking God to show them what they are dealing with.

There is too little time to be wasting it with people who have nothing to do with our future.

Too many saints are making decisions for themselves, when God has provided our great High Priest to help us with these things. What good does it do us to have this connection if we're not using it? We are much too quick to hear the counsel given to us by friends and family members, without first checking to see if our great High Priest agrees. No wonder we are so far behind with our dreams and goals! We have listened to other counselors and not to our great High Priest. We have made too many decisions without first going to the throne room.

So this is another of the downsides to success, another disadvantage to living progressively. A Christian who continually makes progress runs the risk of allowing such progress to go to his head. When this happens, it is common for prideful people to begin to limit the time they spend with God. Somehow they become convinced that they brought themselves to this point and that they can take themselves on to their planned destination. They no longer need God or anyone else. That's a very dangerous position to take.

Paul found himself in danger of being exalted in pride. He was receiving so many great revelations from God, and God was doing so many great things for him that his spirit was in danger of being overwhelmed with self-importance. It was in that moment that the thorn in the flesh was given to him, and this kept his feet on the ground. He had been close to the point of exalting himself and thinking more highly of himself than he ought.

God saw the mistake Paul was about to make and mercifully stepped in, allowing a messenger of Satan to come and buffet him. That gave him reason to return to the throne room of God every day. What a caring God! What a great High Priest! He is enabling us, and we are *Surviving the Crisis.*

CHAPTER 10

KEEPING YOUR FEET ON THE GROUND

And lest I should be exalted above measure by the abundance of the revelations, a thorn in the flesh was given to me, a messenger of Satan to buffet me, lest I be exalted above measure. Concerning this thing I pleaded with the Lord three times that it might depart from me. And He said to me, "My grace is sufficient for you, for My strength is made perfect in weakness." Therefore, most gladly I will rather boast in my infirmities, that the power of Christ may rest upon me. Therefore I take pleasure in infirmities, in reproaches, in needs, in persecutions, in distresses, for Christ's sake. For when I am weak, then I am strong. 2 Corinthians 12:7-10

God has not blessed us just so that we can become pompous and arrogant and begin to look down on those who are not yet at our level of achievement. This is another type of crisis, and is the reason that He sometimes sends a thorn in the flesh our way. It is important for us to understand such thorns.

Certain questions need to be asked: Where does this thing come from? Why is it in our lives? Who is responsible for it? And can we look forward to getting rid of it any time soon?

Paul said that his thorn in the flesh came to him from God and was a means of preventing him from becoming proud. He hadn't ask for this, and it wasn't on his prayer list. It was a messenger of Satan, but it was given to Paul by God Himself.

Although we don't know exactly what Paul's thorn was, it is apparent from what he did say that it was something that tormented him, nagged at him, and frustrated him, and we know that because he prayed several times for it to be removed. Whatever it was that worked negatively on him was there to constantly remind him: "You're not all that."

If anybody in the New Testament had bragging rights, it was Paul. He was responsible for about two thirds of the New Testament writings. Obviously, he had a serious connection with God, for (as we have seen) the Bible says that no scripture was recorded unless it was inspired by God and entrusted to holy men of God.

Paul did have bragging rights, but God said to him, "Hold on now. I have blessed you, Paul, and you have made much progress. You have a good testimony, but let Me now give you a very special gift—a thorn in the flesh. This will help you."

God is serious about you getting where you need to go, and because of that He will bless you and help you make progress. But He will also make sure that you have another gift that is compatible with your level of blessing. This thing will sometimes rock your world, and it will constantly remind you that you need the Lord. It happens to black people and white people, rich people and poor people, educated people and illiterate people. We all need the Lord to help us in this area of life, no matter the particular level we happen to be on.

Some people who have been single for a long time become proud once they have found a mate, and then they look down on those who are still single. God has to get their feet back on the ground, so He allows something to happen that will disturb them. For instance, a woman might find that her new spouse is having an affair. He has given her many things, among them a nice house and a nice car, but now she has this new cross to bear. That's a thorn in her flesh. She may have no other complaints, but this is a big one.

Keeping Your Feet on the Ground

Some people live in an apartment for many years, and they pray many times a day and always include the prayer that God will give them a house. Once they have a house of their own, their prayer times decrease dramatically, and that's a problem. So, what alternative does God have? He wants your love, so He will cause you to lose your job, and you will get behind on your mortgage payments, and the bank will threaten you with foreclosure on your fine new house.

Three times Paul, such a great man of faith and prayer, was so tormented by his thorn in the flesh that he earnestly sought God for it to depart, and yet God said no. Paul needed this thing. He needed some torment, some nagging, some trouble, so that he would remain humble before God.

> *As bad as a thorn might be, God knows you and what you can bear.*

Paul was asking God to remove the thorn, but God said that the thorn was a special gift, so why should He remove it? It was good for Paul, having a positive purpose, so why should He remove it? In love, He refused.

Let's be clear here. As bad as a thorn might be, God knows you and what you can bear. He will never allow your thorn to be more powerful than you. You may sometimes feel that you can't go on bearing this, but God knows that you can—or He wouldn't have given it to you in the first place.

There is no reason for God to remove your thorn, because His grace is sufficient for you to overcome it, and you need that proper alignment of positions—Him as the Lord and you as His humble servant.

And you *can* bear this thing. Grace only comes from God, but He has enough to go around, and His grace is sufficient.

You might work hard in the church, but the thorn will remain. You might sow many financial seeds, but the thorn will remain. You might get others to join you as prayer partners and together you can "bombard heaven," as the old saying goes, but that won't change it. The thorn will remain. Anointed people might pray for you, and their anointing might be powerful enough to break yokes and remove burdens, but that won't change anything. Your thorn will remain. This is a gift from God, and when He gave it to you, He knew exactly what He was doing. So He will not relent unless and until the purpose for the thorn is accomplished in you. The only solution to a thorn in the flesh is the grace to bear it joyfully and to ride out the storm it produces.

Once Paul realized what he was up against, he stopped complaining about his thorn in the flesh and stopped begging God to take it way. Instead, he started thanking God for His all-sufficient grace. He now knew that even when he was weak, he was strong because of God's grace. Grace alone moved him from the weak category into the strong category, and, with God's grace, he could make it through every day.

And with God's grace, you can make it too. Tell yourself so. Remind yourself that you have enough to make it. God's grace is sufficient for *you*, and it will pull *you* out of the darkest hole, lift you out of the lowest pit, and place you on your feet in front of all your enemies.

God's grace will help you learn how to be content with what you have until you can do better. His grace will cause you to move from glory to glory. His grace is sufficient, so defy the thorn in your flesh and start praising God for His grace. Give Him the glory right now with that thorn still in your flesh.

Speak to your thorn today and tell it: "Thorn, do your job well. Go ahead. Keep me humble. Keep my feet on the ground. Keep me connected to my Father. Keep me focused. Do whatever you have to do to accomplish all that."

Once you know that the thorn is not going anywhere and you stop wasting your time praying for God to remove it, you can make some real progress. The thorn will not be removed, but God will give you grace to face it and prevail, so that you can get to the next level He has for you.

Grace will help you! Grace will keep you! God's grace is sufficient for you and will keep you *Surviving the Crisis*.

PART III

SURVIVING THE TESTS OF LIFE

CHAPTER 11

WHAT A LOT OF GOOD A LITTLE AFFLICTION CAN DO

For you, O God, have tested us;
You have refined us as silver is refined.
You brought us into the net;
You laid afflictions on our backs.
You have caused men to ride over our heads;
We went through fire and through water;
But You brought us out to rich fulfillment.   Psalm 66:10-12

I am always amazed at what a lot of good a little affliction, a current crisis, can do in the life of a believer, even a seasoned believer. God, our Creator and Sustainer, always has a purpose in mind when He permits us to go through periods of unfruitfulness, seasons of struggle, trials and tribulations, moments of affliction, times of testings, periods of persecutions—whatever you would prefer to call the difficult experiences that so often come our way.

Some of the things we go through are not meant to be changed, and even if we ask God to change them many times, the answer will always be the same. We are not anointed as believers to change everything that confronts us, but we are called upon to outlive it. Trials and tribulations, persecutions and afflictions, if borne in the right way, can often open the doors to us for a much better way of life.

Let's face it, although we are saved, life is a challenge, and each of us has his own cross to bear. Every one of us has his own pain to endure, and, without a doubt, each of us has his own obstacles to overcome, his own tests to pass. But what is not always immediately understood is that every adversity that we go through in life is both necessary and important to our life's work and the fulfillment of our ultimate destiny. If nothing else, each challenge we face serves as an exercise to gain strength for the next leg of our journey. Some people collapse during a difficult journey because they have failed to exercise enough beforehand. Hopefully that will not be our fate.

> *Adversity and affliction should be received as vehicles that compel us to look deeply into ourselves to see the new lessons we need to learn.*

Adversity and affliction should be received as vehicles that compel us to look deeply into ourselves to see the new lessons we need to learn. As believers, our faith is really all that we have, and a faith that cannot be tested is a faith that cannot be trusted.

Each of us must face the reality, first that our faith must be tested, and second that we don't have the privilege of determining the test. That's God's prerogative.

But that's not a problem, for God is just, and He knows exactly what each of us is capable of enduring. He will never be found wanting when it comes to the care of our souls, and He knows how to test us on our particular level of maturity, or spiritual capacity.

When we are tested, God can't respond for us. He's not being tested; we are. He can't provide the test and also give us the answers. What would that prove? Like a good professor in the classroom, He may indeed remain silent while the test is being conducted.

This may explain why, at some intervals of our lives, while we are encountering severe trials, we don't hear from God. He seems to be oddly silent. That's normal, for it is testing time. For just a moment, He must step back and allow us to complete the test on our own. Otherwise, we would be cheating, and He never allows that.

When we are not undergoing tests, we hear from God frequently. He speaks to us all day long and even sometimes wakes us up in the night to say something important to us. But when the test is in progress, He is nowhere to be found. At one point, Job wondered just where God was, and you have probably had the same thought. Now you know the answer.

A teacher is not empowered to give the answers during an exam. If the teacher gave the answers, no one could determine whether or not the students were really learning. The responsibility of the teacher is to teach, and then when he or she has completed the instruction, it's the student's turn. The teacher may warn the students to prepare for an exam on a certain day, and he or she might review the material covered in the course of the class, but that's as far as a teacher can go. It's up to the student to study the assigned material and to prepare in any other way possible for the upcoming exam, so that when he (or she) arrives in the examination room, he is well prepared and can show what he has learned.

While the test is going on, the teacher, although he or she is present in the examination room, always remains silent. Silence is called for because this is not a time for instruction; it is time for testing. To me, that sounds very much like what God does with us.

As pastor and bishop of the people, it is my duty to teach, but when I'm done, I then sit back and watch what the people will do with the teaching. I can teach them, but I cannot live life for them.

I can teach them, but I cannot take their tests for them. In this respect, they are wholly on their own.

There are times in all of our lives when events hit us so hard that we are left doing one of several unhelpful things. Some of us say things we shouldn't say, some of us go places we shouldn't go and do things we shouldn't do, and most of us start rebuking the devil (who has nothing to do with the situation at all). The sad reality is that many believers cannot handle times of testing—especially when they are given by surprise, like a pop quiz.

A pop quiz is one that we're not expecting. It hasn't been announced, and we have had no opportunity to do any special study or other preparation for it. Teachers use pop quizzes to see who is learning and who is just sleeping through a class. But the nature of such a quiz terrifies us. Are we ready for it? Well, there's no way to know until the test is actually conducted and the resulting grades are in.

So the first important truth we learn from all of this is that God, as our great Teacher, has to permit us to be periodically tested. Temptation comes from Satan, but tests come from God. He uses such tests to analyze our progress and our readiness (or lack of readiness) for further steps in Him.

Would we blame the devil for a pop quiz given by a teacher at school? Surely not. Then we should also not blame the devil for the spiritual tests that come our way. God is their author, and He knows precisely what He is doing when He allows them.

God often speaks something to us far in advance of our needing to use it. When He does this, He is setting our eyes on a certain goal so that we will prepare for it. He never does anything that could confuse us, and He never wastes our time. When He releases a word to us, if we don't need it at that moment, we soon will. We must take hold of it, consider its implications, and then prepare for its fulfillment. And, we must also prepare to be tested on it.

What A Lot of Good a Little Affliction Can Do

Like Mary, the mother of Jesus, hide God's words in your heart:

But Mary kept all these things and pondered them in her heart.
Luke 2:19

When some sermons are preached, we should act upon them immediately, but others should be tucked away in our hearts for a future time. It might be for next week, next month, or next year or even further in the future. Then we must get ready to be tested on this new material.

When temptations come, we can know that it's the devil's way of trying to destroy us, but when tests come, it's God's way of trying to advance us. Since Satan is such a great deceiver, he always tries to make us feel that experiencing a test means that we are out of the will of God, backslidden, lost, gone astray. He tries to make us feel that we have sinned and that God doesn't love us anymore.

"Why else would you be going through this?" he gloats. But now you know the truth. Now you know exactly why trials and tests are coming your way. It's only a test, and you can come through it with flying colors.

Satan always tries to take credit for your test, and he does that to focus your attention on him, not on advancement in God (the object of the test in the first place). If you spend most of your time rebuking the devil and taking authority over him, you won't have time to prepare for what is ahead.

A lot of the rebuking people are doing these days is an exercise in futility. Satan has nothing to do with the tests we're going through. If it were a temptation, then he might, but with a test, never. The problem is that many don't know the difference. And the people around us often don't know the difference either. They try to deliver us and set us free, but it won't work, because tests are crucial to our forward progress, and they come from God Himself.

Stop spending so much time rebuking the devil and spend more time talking to God about His plans for your future. Ask Him to show you why you are experiencing this great trial and what He hopes to accomplish in you through it.

Some people are under the mistaken impression that once a person is saved and starts living holy, he or she automatically has all the answers to life's questions. Being saved is only the beginning of our journey, and if we already had all the answers, we would never need to be tested.

None of us has yet arrived at perfection, and each of us has at least one thing that still troubles us. I can predict with certainty that more times of testing will come to your life. There can be no doubt about that fact. It doesn't matter how anointed you are, times of testing will come to you. It doesn't matter how close you are to Jesus, times of testing will come.

Such times of testing were never intended to do you harm, discourage you, or knock you down. To the contrary, they are to let you know how close you are to getting another spiritual degree. And the closer you get, the harder and more frequent the tests will become.

When students are tested at the end of grading periods, it signals that they are about to complete their current course of studies. The tests they take serve the purpose of determining whether or not they are ready to move on to another level.

Tests, then, are serious business, and if a student has just gone through the motions and not really studied or listened well during lectures, how can he or she expect to do well on a test? Those who have played around while the professor was teaching, skipped classes, or failed to complete assignments will not be deemed worthy of elevation. They will surely fail the test.

Sometimes in preparing ourselves for what God is about to do, we only need to look at what He has already done. In this regard,

What A Lot of Good a Little Affliction Can Do

Psalm 66 is very helpful to us. The psalmist clearly knew God in His testings and realized that it was all for his refinement.

But if God already knows everything, why does He have to test us in this way? He doesn't. You're right. He already knows. So the testing is for our benefit, not His.

As far back as the book of Genesis, God began to prove men:

> *Now it came to pass after these things that God tested Abraham ... .*   Genesis 22:1

Abraham became the father of our faith, but before he could reach that exalted position, he was severely tested. And God hasn't changed his method of operations. He has always tested men and women, and He always will.

So, why are we so fearful of tests? We were like that in school too, but tests proved to be the way we progressed from grade to grade and eventually graduated. In this way, tests worked to our benefit.

Times of testing were never intended to do you harm, discourage you, or knock you down

Like many, I was not always a great student, and I was guilty of having to cram at the last minute for exams. Although I did try to retain as much information as I could from what we were being taught, I was especially adamant about preparing well for tests. I really wanted to do well on them, and I have maintained that same attitude about the tests of life.

How do we prepare for tests in real life? Our daily personal devotional time with God should be a time in which He can pour into us. Then the corporate gathering of the saints, on the days in which we join together in the House of God, represent another important moment for us to learn and grow. At these times, each of us should be prayed-up, fired-up, and ready for what God is about to say to us through His servants. Our minds should be clear, and our spirits should be in tune with God. Then we should remain attentive as God speaks through His earthly priests.

Some have mistakenly abandoned the habit of regular church attendance, believing that they can receive all that they need from God at home. What God speaks to each of us personally is important, but what He speaks to us corporately is equally important. There is no substitute for regular church attendance, and we must not kid ourselves into thinking that we can get what we need some other way. Many saints are failing because of this misconception. Skipping classes is always reflected in poor performance on tests.

Some, when they miss church, call a friend and ask what the Bible lesson was about so that they can study it on their own. This shortcut will not make up for their missed attendance. Nothing will, and nothing can. What God does in the assembly of the saints, as He feeds us all on our respective spiritual levels, is mysterious and miraculous. You need it, and I do too. So don't miss it.

Some people call me, saying that they had to miss a certain session for one reason or another and ask me to summarize what was taught. It is nearly impossible to go back and recreate the atmosphere in which the Holy Spirit moved, as deep called to deep and our spirits were enriched with manna from on high. I can try, but it will rarely have the same effect.

When we are pursuing an education, we invest in textbooks that usually contain much of the information we need to learn to take our tests and graduate. Although we, as Christians, have our Bibles, which are full of great truths, the way the Holy Spirit presents these truths to us in the corporate setting is difficult to duplicate in private. And not everything we teach in church is in the Bible. Our teaching is Bible-based, but it includes our personal experiences and other illustrations from life.

In a college context, if you do a good job of reviewing the book, you can make a decent grade on the test, but in real life, it doesn't work that way. The closest thing we have come up with to approximate actually being in church is our recorded sermon cassettes. Investing in them, we have found, and then listening to them again, perhaps several times, pays off. Still, this cannot duplicate the live experience of actually being in the service. It would be like comparing seeing a blockbuster movie on the big screen of a large theater and seeing it later through video cassette or DVD on a small-screen television. It's the same movie production, but there is a world of difference in how it impacts you. Invest in some of the recorded messages of your pastor and teacher, but don't stop going to the house of God to experience His awesome presence in person.

I often tell the members of our ministry that they must assume that since God knows all things, there must be a reason He brought us all together. If He truly connected us in this way, there must be something in them and in me that required this joining. For their part, they must have needed the kind of messages God gives me, and that could explain the reason that the first time they attended my church and heard me preach, their hearts leaped inside them. A spirit connection was made, and we always need to protect and promote such a connection. God has set His servants in place for just such a purpose.

So, who tests us? It is God. And who is it, according to the text, who refines us. It is God.

Silver is refined by the application of heat. It has to go through the fire. And it is rare that a believer receives everything God has for him or her without first going through fire. Before you can be trusted, your faith must be tested. Zechariah the prophet wrote:

I will bring the one third through the fire,
Will refine them as silver is refined,
And test them as gold is tested.
They will call on My name,
And I will answer them.
I will say "This is My people";
And each one will say, "The Lord is my God."

Zechariah 13:9

> *While we're actually in the fire, He [God] may be silent.*

After the refining process is ended, after we have gone through the fire, then God will answer us. While we're actually in the fire, He may be silent. When all is said and done, He will be our God, and we will be His people. This is the goal; this is the purpose. Be faithful in the test, and know that the outcome will be wonderful beyond words.

The psalmist continued: *"You brought us into the net"* (Psalm 66:11). When a net is cast over an animal, the animal is trapped. When you feel trapped, therefore, don't automatically take for granted the fact that the devil has done it. God is sometimes responsible for our feeling trapped. When it looks like we can't make any progress, and we are hemmed in on every side, it may indeed be God's work. He is testing us.

"You laid afflictions on our backs" (Psalm 66:11). Who did it? It was God, and all this time we've been giving the devil credit. As members of the Body of Christ and citizens of the Kingdom of God, we have passed the stage when Satan can willfully afflict us. If some affliction is coming to us, it's because God has permitted it.

Because we are full of God and full of His Word, the devil and his demons are now afraid of us. Most of us haven't learned that fact well enough yet. What Satan can effectively do to us now is very limited. Therefore when we see something seemingly wrong happening in our lives, we must pause to consider if we might be out of order (God's order), and if not, what God is trying to teach us by this current trial.

Jesus was crucified, and we automatically assume that Satan had a hand in His death, but, in reality, Satan didn't have the authority or the power to take Jesus' life. Jesus Himself said:

> *Therefore My Father loves Me, because I lay down My life that I may take it again. No one takes it from Me, but I lay it down of Myself. I have power to lay it down, and I have power to take it again. This command I have received from My Father.*
>
> John 10:17-18

Jesus laid down His life. No one—not even Satan—had the power to take it from Him. The death of Jesus was the doing of our Heavenly Father. He brought His Son to die so that we all might live. Only He had that power.

There is more. The psalmist continued: *"You have caused men to ride over our heads"* (Psalm 66:12). Sometimes, when men take advantage of us, God is behind it. He is testing us, so we must not blame Satan. No amount of rebuking and binding will change what is happening in these moments. God is testing us, and we must complete the test. He will see if we are easily crushed by what men do to us, or if we have learned to look to the hills for strength and help:

> *I will lift up my eyes to the hills—*
> *From whence comes my help?*
> *My help comes from the LORD,*
> *Who made heaven and earth.*
>
> Psalm 121:1-2

When some person opposes your promotion and your salary increase and tries to keep you at the low end of the totem pole, you can know that it is not Satan's work, but God's. He is testing you. When some individual tries to make you look bad in the eyes of the owner of the business or in the eyes of your supervisor or co-workers, know that God is at work. He is testing you. Don't take it personally.

Tests don't go on forever. There is an end to them. The psalmist declared: *"We went through fire and through water; but You brought us out to rich fulfillment"* (Psalm 66:12). It is God who takes you into a test, and it is God who brings you through it. And when He does, it will be *"to rich fulfillment."*

It is not Satan who tests us, but God. It is not Satan who refines us in the fire, but God. It is not Satan who brings us into the net, but God. It is not Satan who lays affliction upon us, but God. It is not Satan who causes men to *"ride over"* us, but God. And it is not Satan who brings us out of the test, but God.

God always brings us out of trials and tests, so why are we sometimes so frustrated while they are in progress? He has a good purpose for our testing, His desire is to lift us to a new level, and we cannot move from here to there without first being tested. So stop feeling frustrated and realize that God is bringing you out.

What you are currently dealing with was not designed to kill you; it was designed to bring you to graduation day. As you have moved up in grade level, the work has grown progressively more difficult, and the tests have grown increasingly demanding. Don't be frustrated with this fact. You are preparing for something great, so you can't expect to always go through first-grade tests. If each level seems to be more difficult than the last, know that this is perfectly normal and that you are more capable at each level to face whatever comes and to overcome it.

The same God who was with you in the lower level of testing is with you now, and He knows that you are ready for this next level (or He would not have allowed the test to come to you in the first place). Hold on, child of God, this is just a test. Don't fight it. If you fight the test, you're fighting against your promotion to the next level.

Since it is God who tests us and refines us, puts us into the net, brings affliction upon us, and allows men to ride over us, we must trust Him to bring us out. Tests are always of rather short duration, and then they're over and past. You can begin celebrating now, for God has promised to bring you out, and He will. You are *Surviving the Crisis*.

CHAPTER 12

HE'S BRINGING YOU OUT

For you, O God, have tested us;
You have refined us as silver is refined.
You brought us into the net;
You laid afflictions on our backs.
You have caused men to ride over our heads;
We went through fire and through water;
But You brought us out to rich fulfillment.   Psalm 66:10-12

Surely all of us, as members of the family of God, have, at some point or another, come to recognize that there are times of testing on this journey—crises, if you will. As we have seen, these testing times do not come from Satan, as most of us had formerly supposed. Satan tempts us with the intention of trying to cause us to go astray, but God tests us with the intention of promoting us further in His Kingdom.

Even Jesus was tempted. Both Matthew and Luke record that temptation. Jesus was led by the Spirit out to a wilderness area, and there, as He was alone in extended prayer and fasting, Satan came to attack Him. But God even had a purpose in this, and Satan did not win the battle that day.

Abraham was tested, as were the other patriarchs, and the psalmist was also sorely tested. It doesn't matter how anointed you are or how close to God you may be at the time, testing times will come. This doesn't mean that you are away from God or that He no longer loves you. To the contrary. Testing times come because you *are* walking with God.

The devil tempts you to drive you away from God, but God releases tests into your life to draw you closer to Him. The two assignments are very different, so when something happens to us, we need to know and understand what we're dealing with.

It is God who tests us and refines us as silver, and the prophet Zechariah spoke of this refining process. It is one which requires being subjected to fire. So when God is working in your life to refine you, don't expect to be in a comfortable situation. When God wants to make something wonderful out of your life, He squeezes you, putting you into tight places, and He lets you go through the fire. In the end, He will bring you out into *"rich fulfillment."*

When God puts you into a tight place and begins to allow circumstances to squeeze you, you must be careful how you react. Instead of realizing what is happening and where God is taking you through this whole process, you might, as many do, spend all of your time rebuking the devil. But he has absolutely nothing to do with this matter. It is God who is doing this thing.

God causes men to *"ride over our heads."* I interpret that to mean that they will be unkind to us, or take advantage of us. Once in a while, God will place some people in your life who will seem to have an anointing to frustrate you and walk all over you. It is important in those moments to know that these people are on assignment from God to deal with you on that level. But even as He allows men to frustrate you for a time, God has already prepared for your deliverance. He will always receive glory through the experience, and you will be a better person for it.

God tests us, He refines us, He brings us into the net, He lays afflictions on our backs, and he causes men to ride over us, but He also brings us out. That is His assurance. When we know this, it makes it much easier for us to relax in the midst of the trial and to rest in the assurance that because of what He has for us to do, God will always bring us out. So, just let God do what He has to do in you to prepare you for the greater thing. If He has promised to bring you out, what are you so worried about?

While I was preaching at the church my brother pastors in Miami, Florida, the revelation came to me that God never brings us out of one thing unless He has a plan to take us into something else. Did He save us just to save us? No. Did He save us just so that we can go to heaven? No. He saved us so that we can glorify Him here on the earth. When He works miracles in our lives and brings us out of difficult situations, He is exalted and "looks good" in the eyes of men. So He brings us out to take us in.

> *When God brings you through some test, you're now ready to move into a place of greater blessing, something you couldn't previously handle.*

Please understand and accept this important fact. If God is bringing you out of something, He's taking you into something else. "Into what?" is the important question. The psalmist assures us that when God has tried us, then He brings us out into a wealthy place, a place of abundance, a place of rich fulfillment, a place of overflowing supply.

When God brings you through some test, you're now ready to move into a place of greater blessing, something you couldn't previously handle. This was the purpose of the test in the first place. This was the purpose of the fire, the purpose of the afflictions, the purpose of men riding over your head. God's getting you ready for greatness, and the greater your coming blessing the more you must be tested in preparation for it.

Before God gets you where you're going, you have to be tested.

You have to go through some fire. Just before He takes you into your new position of blessing, He just might have to let men ride over you. He might have to lay affliction on your back or place you in a standstill position for a while. None of this is intended to discourage you. God wants you to experience His delivering power and to know for sure who it is who takes you in.

Knowing now what we know about all that the psalmist had to go through, it is very interesting to look back and see how he began this psalm:

> *Make a joyful shout to God, all the earth!*
> *Sing out the honor of His name;*
> *Make His praise glorious.*
> *Say to God,*
> *"How awesome are Your works!*
> *Through the greatness of Your power*
> *Your enemies shall submit themselves to You."* Psalm 66:1-3

Despite all that he had been through, the psalmist began the song with a period of celebration. He wants to *"shout to God,"* to *"sing out the honor of His name,"* and to *"make His praise glorious."* He wants to tell God how *"awesome"* His works are. That doesn't sound to me like a man who is discouraged and defeated.

No, the trials we face should never defeat us, and if we go into them with the proper attitude, we will come through them easily by the power of our God. And, like the psalmist, we can sing and shout to God when we understand the purpose of life's trials and when we face them squarely with Him on our side. If we were to constantly dwell on the afflictions and sufferings of verses 10 through 12, we could easily become discouraged, but if we dwell instead on the praises of God, nothing can discourage us.

The shout to God of verse one is to be a *"joyful"* one, and how can we do that after passing through so many trials, or while still going through those trials? It is accomplished by focusing on the end result, God's purpose for the test, and what He will soon be bringing us into. So, when you praise God, don't just make noise. Get His joy into your spirit.

Rather than dwell upon your current difficult situation, whatever it happens to be right now, you should tell God how glorious and awesome He is. Do it joyfully and exuberantly. If you are near people who cannot or should not be disturbed, then move somewhere else so that you can be free to celebrate. Find a private place of jubilation and position yourself for praise. If now is not a convenient time to do it, then make a commitment to do it just as soon as it *is* convenient. Our God is worthy of all praise.

The Lord has shown me that He looks differently on our praise that is a result of receiving some gift or blessing from Him than He does on praise that is offered out of our pain and suffering. When we have nothing, when we are still in the battlefield trenches, or when we are still in the midst of our trial, God takes note that our praises to Him in these situations are exceptional, and He rewards us accordingly. Get into the habit of praising God, not only because of what He has already done, but also because of what you know He has promised to do and *will* do in the future. He will bring you out and take you into a place of *"rich fulfillment."*

The psalmist encouraged us to *"sing out the honor of His name."* It is important that we understand God's name, because the name we use for Him always reveals something about His character. So, when we understand His names, we can attach the proper name to our particular need, based upon the revelation of His nature, and then we can *"sing out the honor of His name."* This helps us to have our current need met more quickly.

But before that need is met, you must begin to praise Him, sing the honor of His name, and tell Him how awesome He is. Praise

Him in anticipation of the end result. Let God know that you appreciate what He is doing in your life—even though you sometimes don't understand it and struggle with it. Let Him know that because you are coming to realize the purpose of the things that confront you in daily life, you better understand just where He is going with all of this. Let Him know that you realize that He loves you and wants the very best for your life.

> *Keep focusing on God and keep praising Him until your test has run its course, and you have been victorious once more.*

Periodically, pause to talk to God about your situation. Tell Him how you see it, and ask Him to let you see it from His perspective. Even though your situation is not yet resolved, you know that He has power to fix it— *"Your enemies shall submit themselves to You."* Keep focusing on God and keep praising Him until your test has run its course, and you have been victorious once more.

Let God know that you are aware of the mighty power that rests in His hands, that you know that at any moment He chooses He can deliver you from your situation, and that as the Almighty God, everything about the future is in His hands. And let Him know that you trust Him with your life and you trust His plan for your future. Then thank Him for the tests that are necessary to your maturity.

All enemies will have to submit themselves to Him, and enemies come in many forms. Sometimes our enemies are people, but often they are something else. Sickness is an enemy; poverty is an enemy; oppression is an enemy; discouragement and depression are enemies. When we shout to God joyfully, sing out the honor His name, make His praise glorious, and tell Him how awesome

He is, the result will be that all of His enemies will submit themselves to Him.

If you are under attack from any direction, it is not by chance that you have picked up this book to read. This is a divine appointment with God. Your enemies are about to submit to you, and you are about to enter into the thing God has been preparing you for.

In the Spirit, I see sickness falling off of those who believe. I see poverty moving aside because God's name is being exalted. Believe with me right now.

Run, Sickness, run! You can no longer afflict this child of God.

Run, Disease, run!

Back up, cancer!

Run, High Blood Pressure!

It is time to go, Depression! God's name is great in the life of this individual.

Friend, if you are tired of the enemies of God destroying your life, begin to praise and magnify the Lord right now where you are. And when you do, watch the enemies in your life begin to fall at your feet. Then you can *really* celebrate because the battle is over, and the victory has been won. You are destined to continue *Surviving the Crisis.*

CHAPTER 13

WHEN THE TEST IS FINALLY OVER

Come and see the works of God;
He is awesome in His doing toward the sons of men.

Psalm 66:5

We have concluded from Psalm 66 (verses 10 and 11) that it is God who tests us (sends various crises our way). He often does this by putting us through the fire to refine us just as silver is refined. It is God who brings us into the net, the net representing something that traps you so that you seemingly cannot move to the right or left, forward or backward. It is God who lays afflictions on our backs and causes men to ride over us. But it is also God who brings us out, and He brings us out to *"rich fulfillment."*

The King James Version of the Bible calls this place of *"rich fulfillment"* *"a wealthy place."* We usually think of money when we call someone "wealthy," but there is a wealth to be found in many other areas of life. It could be a wealth of good health, a wealth of relationships, a wealth of family life, a wealth of success in a career, or any other wealth. You can have wealth in any and every aspect of your life, and this is what God wants for you.

But in order to qualify for God to take you into *"a wealthy place,"* you first have to come *out of* something, and before God brings you out of something, He has to put you *through* something. That's the part none of us likes. But He has the right to test us, and His tests are necessary to our advancement.

135

Testing fires come to us periodically, and only God can say when one is due. Each test is custom designed to let us know where we stand in God's Kingdom and to prepare us and qualify us for a new level. How exciting!

As we have already observed, God knows all things, and so He knows what your reaction will be to any given test. He gives it to you anyway, because He wants you to know what you are capable of, and He wants you to see what He is working out in your life.

> *Taking God's tests is a way for you to mature and advance.*

Taking God's tests is a way for you to mature and advance. It assures proper preparation. It gauges your level of achievement. It validates your faith, your trust level with God, and it gauges the depth of your spiritual strength. And, as we have seen, a faith that cannot be tested is a faith that cannot be trusted.

The devil has very different intentions when he tempts you. He wants to weaken you and, if possible, to bring you down. He wants you to fall in disgrace. He is always up to no good. But don't be unduly concerned about him or the temptations he will send your way. God has promised that nothing will come to you that you are incapable of handling:

> *No temptation has overtaken you except such as is common to man; but God is faithful, who will not allow you to be tempted beyond what you are able, but with the temptation will also make the way of escape, that you may be able to bear it.*
>
> 1 Corinthians 10:13

There are two promised safeguards here. (1) God will not allow you to be tempted beyond your capacity to resist, and (2) He will, with every temptation, provide for you *"the way of escape."* That is wonderful to know.

Tests are totally different from temptations. We will all be tested, but as Spirit-filled people of God, we should not be succumbing to temptation over and over again. This is especially true when we are chosen for any position in the ministry. When we step forward in spiritual leadership, others are looking to us as examples, and how we live from day to day will deeply affect them. The Holy Spirit is always with us in our temptations, just as He is in our times of testing.

When a test is over, and has run its course, we begin to experience some new things. We come into a whole new season in our lives:

> **Come and see the works of God;**
> **He is awesome in His doing toward the sons of men.**
>
> Psalm 66:5

"Come and see." If you have read this far in the book, I believe that you are among those whom God has chosen to take into a new season. I call this new season "the season of *'Come and see!'* " Everything that you have been dealing with up to this moment, all of the tests you have had to endure, all the things you have struggled with and tried to conquer, have come to you because of God and because He has wanted to prepare you for this special season of your life. Let me explain what I mean by this phrase "the season of *'Come and see.'* "

First of all, to me, *"come and see"* represents an immediate action. It means "now," "quickly," "don't hesitate." And this is what God is doing for many.

I realize that if God is bringing you into a season of *"Come and see,"* it means that He will have to do something quickly to free you from the circumstances that have bound you and kept you from making progress. But He can do that. Doing something suddenly is not hard for God. And if you're ready for a new season, He is too.

Quickly put your affairs in order, because you don't have much time. Things are going to begin to happen very suddenly now. When this current test is over, you can expect God to move in a magnanimous way in your life and to do it quickly. You will have to say to many in passing, "I don't have time to explain. You'll just have to come and see for yourself." And that is the second part of the *"come and see"* season. It is a time for renewed testimonies that impact others.

Because you have been tried and tested, because you have experienced being caught in the net, because afflictions were laid on you, because people were allowed to ride over your head, and because you came through the fire and through the water (when, in reality, no one expected you to make it), you're personally ready for some great blessings. It's moving time. This is a new season in your life. And this new season will not only affect you; it will affect many others around you.

Many people looked at you, saw all that you were dealing with, and concluded that there was no way you could come out of the mess you were in. You were so crushed that only a miracle could have kept you alive and standing. Some had already pronounced a benediction upon you. The next time they see you, they will be so surprised, but you'll hardly have time to stop and explain it all to them. It's all going to happen very suddenly.

Things are about to happen so quickly all around you that you will actually find no logical explanation that could satisfy others for what has just taken place in your life. The best you will be able to do is to say to them, "Just come and see."

"Come and see what the Lord has done."

"Come and see how He made a way."

When the Test Is Finally Over

"Come and see how He brought me out."

"Come and see."

Many will have difficulty believing what they now see because the last time they saw you, you were already "out for the count." You were so deeply in debt that you had almost lost everything. And, if it hadn't been for the grace and mercy of God, you would have lost everything. As a result of your financial loss, you probably would have lost your family, and you may have lost your mind. The last person everyone expected to have a joyous testimony is you, and they will be amazed when they hear you say, *"Come and see."*

The people around you thought you would never rise to this level, because not too very long ago, you were asking for their help. You needed a favor just to exist. Now you can joyfully tell them, *"Come and see."*

This *"come and see"* realm is the place God is preparing to take you next, and, if you're not yet convinced of it, you need to prophesy to yourself today, and say, "Self, you're headed for an unprecedented season of *'come and see.'* Get ready for what is coming."

The Bible assures us of the power of agreement, so today I come into agreement with you for this blessing upon your life. Let it happen, and let it happen soon.

The psalmist continued. He spoke not only of the *"come and see"* blessing, but also of the *"come and hear"* blessing :

> *Come and hear, all you who fear God,*
> *And I will declare what He has done for my soul.* Psalm 66:16

This is the time for all saints to make their blessings known. Everyone seems to be "coming out of the closet" with their evil life-styles, and it is time that God's people stop hiding what He has done for them. Tell everyone you know: "God's been so good to me." Tell them how He has made a way for you, how He has opened doors that were once shut in your face. Tell everyone who will listen. Declare the goodness of the Lord everywhere.

You may not feel like your testimony has been all that powerful, but it's about to receive a supercharge; it's about to be refreshed and renewed. Soon, you will not need to speak only of things gone by; you will be able to tell what God is doing for you in the here and now. He is about to radically change your life and, with it, your testimony.

Earlier the psalmist had said:

> *He turned the sea into dry land;*
> *They went through the river on foot.*
> *There we will rejoice in Him.* Psalm 66:6

The New International Version of the Bible says it this way:

> *He turned the sea into the dry land,*
> *they passed through the waters on foot—*
> *Come, let us rejoice in Him.* Psalms 66:6, NIV

So, here's the deal: God is taking you into a season of *"Come and see,"* into a season of *"Come and hear,"* but before you can go out and proudly tell others, *"Come and see,"* and *"Come and hear,"* your own life has to be in order. Your own spirit has to be right. You need to develop a spirit of celebration and praise—not just for what is coming, but for who God is and for what He has done to bring you to this place.

First rejoice alone, and then ask others to join you, people who are capable of taking a faith walk with you. Say to them, *"Come, let us rejoice in Him."* When they ask you what you're rejoicing about, answer them, "We're rejoicing over the season that is dawning—our season of *"come and see,"* our season of *"come and hear."*

There is strength in spiritual numbers, just as there is in physical numbers. Jesus said:

> *Again I say to you that if two of you agree on earth concerning anything that they ask, it will be done for them by My Father in heaven. For where two or three are gathered together in My name, I am there in the midst of them.* Matthew 18:19-20

"It will be done." What a powerful promise! Jeremiah knew the power of the Lord to work wonders in the earth:

> *Ah, Lord God! Behold, You have made the heavens and the earth by Your great power and outstretched arm. There is nothing too hard for You.* Jeremiah 32:17

This is a word worth tucking away in your spirit at this important juncture of your life. There is absolutely and positively nothing too hard for God to do. Never allow the devil to fool you with how bad things look at the moment. If you listen to him, you may cancel out the good things that are coming your way. No matter how bad things look, there is nothing too hard for God.

The prophet received more revelation in this regard:

You may not feel like your testimony has been all that powerful, but it's about to receive a supercharge; it's about to be refreshed and renewed.

SURVIVING THE CRISIS

Then the word of the Lord came to Jeremiah saying, "Behold I am the Lord, the God of all flesh. Is there anything too hard for Me?   Jeremiah 32:26-27

It's a rhetorical question, and we all know the answer. There is nothing too hard for the Lord. That means that your present situation should not prevent you from rejoicing over the promises of God and over what you expect Him to do for you any day now. It is in the atmosphere of rejoicing that the Spirit of God moves. Let the release come.

Rejoicing despite every test is the theme of Psalm 66. The psalmist speaks of a time when *"all the earth"* would worship the Lord and *"sing praises"* to Him. What you are doing now will help to bring that time into being. For now, you're praising God in faith, praising Him prophetically. You are thanking Him for what He has not yet done. Yes, we do thank God for everything He has done for us in the past and what He is doing for us today, but we must also thank Him for the truly awesome things that are about to take place in the earth and in our personal lives.

Rejoice in the Lord. He's bringing you out of tests, so that He can take you into richness. Having gone through the fire was not in vain. Bearing affliction was not in vain. Having people take advantage of you was not in vain. God is now bringing you out of all that, and because He found you to be faithful in every test, He is now taking you into new realms in Him.

He is about to refresh and renew your testimony so that you can tell everyone around you, *"Come and see,"* and *"Come and hear."* He's bringing you out, so that He can bring you into this new season. And it will be done because there's nothing too hard for our God. My friend, you are *Surviving the Crisis*.

CHAPTER 14

TEMPTATION DOES SERVE A GOOD PURPOSE AFTER ALL

Then Jesus was led up by the Spirit into the wilderness to be tempted by the devil.   Matthew 4:1

If we can understand temptation and its purpose (again, a different type of crisis), we can better respond to it when it comes our way. For instance, temptation should never be a cause for self-condemnation. We are all tempted. Even Jesus, as perfect as He was, was tempted.

Let me begin this discussion of temptation by emphasizing the fact that temptation, in and of itself, is neither good nor bad, right nor wrong. Temptation does not work for you, nor does it work against you. Temptation becomes good or bad, right or wrong, based only upon how you respond to it. If you respond to temptation in faith, then each temptation will bring strength into your life and prepare you for the next temptation to come. If you give in to temptation and yield to it, that yielding brings sin and, with it, a built-in weakness to further temptation.

No one is ever disqualified from this race because he or she has been tempted. As a matter of fact, no one is disqualified from this race because they have yielded to temptation. Yielding will adversely affect any believer, but it will not automatically disqualify them. You can be disqualified from this race only by forsaking the Lord and His love for your life—no other way.

Many have been deceived into thinking that temptation is somehow an indication of weakness in our lives, but nothing could be further from the truth. Weak people don't require much temptation. They do the wrong thing regardless. But when we become strong in the Lord, Satan gets concerned and shows up with his temptations to try to bring us down and leave us in a state of confusion. Therefore the higher you go in God, the stronger the temptations will become.

Most of us are familiar with the temptation of Jesus. Some, when they have yielded to temptation, use the excuse, "Well, even Jesus was tempted." But there is a great difference between being tempted and yielding to temptation. Yes, Jesus was tempted, but He did not yield to that temptation—not even for a moment.

> *There is a great difference between being tempted and yielding to temptation.*

Matthew began his narrative of the temptation of Jesus in this way: *"Then Jesus..."* *"Then ..."* When? To answer this question, we must look back to the previous chapter. Although it is rather lengthy, reading most of it is beneficial to our understanding of just what happened the day Jesus was tempted:

In those days John the Baptist came preaching in the wilderness of Judea, and saying, "Repent, for the kingdom of heaven is at hand!" For this is he who was spoken of by the prophet Isaiah, saying:

"The voice of one crying in the wilderness:
'Prepare the way of the Lord;
Make His paths straight.' "

Temptation Does Serve a Good Purpose After All

And John himself was clothed in camel's hair, with a leather belt around his waist; and his food was locusts and wild honey. Then Jerusalem, all Judea, and all the region around the Jordan went out to him and were baptized by him in the Jordan, confessing their sins.

But when he saw many of the Pharisees and Sadducees coming to his baptism, he said to them, "Brood of vipers! Who warned you to flee from the wrath to come? Therefore bear fruits worthy of repentance, and do not think to say to yourselves, 'We have Abraham as our father.' For I say to you that God is able to raise up children to Abraham from these stones.

"And even now the ax is laid to the root of the trees. Therefore every tree which does not bear good fruit is cut down and thrown into the fire. I indeed baptize you with water unto repentance, but He who is coming after me is mightier than I, whose sandals I am not worthy to carry. He will baptize you with the Holy Spirit and fire. His winnowing fan is in His hand, and He will thoroughly purge [clean out] His threshing floor, and gather His wheat into the barn; but He will burn up the chaff with unquenchable fire."

Then Jesus came from Galilee to John at the Jordan to be baptized by him. And John tried to prevent Him, saying, "I have need to be baptized by You, and are You coming to me?"

But Jesus answered and said to him, "Permit it to be so now, for thus it is fitting for us to fulfill all righteousness." Then he allowed Him.

Then Jesus, when He had been baptized, came up immediately from the water; and behold, the heavens were opened to Him, and He saw the Spirit of God descending like a dove and alighting upon Him. And suddenly a voice came from heaven saying, "This is My beloved Son, in whom I am well pleased."

SURVIVING THE CRISIS

Then Jesus was led up by the Spirit into the wilderness to be tempted by the devil.   Matthew 3:1-4:1

No sooner had Jesus been baptized, affirmed by His heavenly Father, and released to begin His public ministry here on earth than He was confronted with temptation. Temptation never comes to us when we're making no spiritual progress at all. Those who remain stagnant and make no progress are not tempted in the least. Satan leaves them alone. It is those whom the enemy would like to stop who are bothered with temptation. If you have no desire to want to better yourself, to live righteously, and to walk in the commands of God, very little temptation will come to your life. The devil already has you, so why does he need to expend additional energy on you?

Jesus was born into this world for a purpose. His life here would affect the entire course of human history. He was taken to the Temple in Jerusalem as an infant, and then little is known of His life until He was twelve years of age, and He was again in the Temple in Jerusalem. At this point, He was already baffling the doctors of the Law. They could not understand why a boy of that age was declaring to his parents:

Why did you seek Me? Did you not know that I must be about My Father's business?   Luke 2:49

After this incident, we again don't hear much about Jesus until He was thirty years old, and that's a long time. It was at that age that He was baptized, affirmed (as the voice of the Father was heard from heaven), and anointed to begin His earthy ministry (as the Spirit of God descended upon Him like a dove).

We cannot say that Jesus had never been tempted prior to this moment, but no temptations were recorded in the Bible as being

146

worthy of our attention. He was surely tempted in His early years to do something other than the will of His Father, but it was when He had stepped into this exalted role of ministry that the more severe temptations began.

I trust that no one is naive enough to assume that those who are in ministry are somehow exempt from temptation. How foolish! Would the devil permit men and women to work for God and for the cause of His Kingdom and not make any attempt to pull them down and destroy them? Never. Those who are at the forefront of Christian ministry face even greater enemy attacks. For this reason, it's always a good idea for young people, just starting out in Christian ministry, to move up slowly in leadership, preparing themselves well at each stage for what is to come in the next.

Jesus lived His life in apparent seclusion between the ages of twelve and thirty, choosing to remain out to the public eye until He was anointed by the Father. Some are ordained and anointed for a special task long before they are released for it. Jesus surely knew His purpose for coming to earth. That was made clear to us by what He said in the Temple at the age of twelve. So, if He knew what His purpose in life was, why would He wait so long before getting started with it? Why didn't He just start preaching there in the Temple that day when He was twelve? God has His own timing for everything, and Jesus showed us how important it is to wait until we are affirmed by the Father.

Even though it was the devil who immediately challenged Jesus after His release into the ministry, it was the Spirit who led Him into the wilderness to be tempted. If the Spirit led Him, then temptation must ultimately serve a good purpose in our lives too.

"The wilderness" was a place of isolation, a lonely place, and yet it was to this isolated place that the Spirit led Jesus. And the purpose of the Spirit leading Him there to *"the wilderness"* was *"to be tempted by the devil."*

Again, Jesus had just been baptized, affirmed by His Father, anointed, and released to start His public ministry, and immediately following all of that He was led of the Holy Spirit into the wilderness to be tempted by the devil. This was a prelude to greater things to come.

It appears, from this, that many of us are not handling temptation correctly. Many in the Body of Christ, instead of using temptation as a means of overcoming and moving on to a new level, are giving in to temptation. And if we are yielding to temptation, then our perspective is wrong. We have the ability to rise above every temptation in life, so the fact that many are becoming victims of temptation is very sad indeed.

Jesus, who is our example, was led into temptation for a purpose. It was the devil who tempted Him, but He was led into the temptation by the Spirit of God.

God never tempts us Himself:

> *Let no one say when he is tempted, "I am tempted by God"; for God cannot be tempted by evil, nor does He Himself tempt anyone. But each one is tempted when he is drawn away by his own desires and enticed. Then, when desire has conceived, it gives birth to sin; and sin, when it is full-grown, brings forth death.* James 1:13-15

As we have seen, God tests us, and the devil tempts us, but in both instances, the Holy Spirit is involved. He is with us in our tests, to help us react as we should. And, in the same way, He is with us in our temptations, to see that we react correctly to them. We need never feel alone either in times of trial and testing or in times of temptation. God is always there.

Every time we are tempted, we have the two assurances we mentioned previously: (1) That God would never permit us to face a particular temptation if He knew in advance that we could not over-come it, and (2) that He will always show us a way of escaping the temptation He has allowed us to face.

The devil cannot do anything to us—temptation included—without God's permission and consent. If the devil is assigned to tempt you, he does it only with God's prior consent. That should be a comforting thought. And if this is true—and we know that it is—why should we fear any temptation? Temptation is not the problem. The problem comes when we ignore the urgings of the Spirit, who is always with us in our time of temptation, and will always show us *"the way of escape"* He has provided for that particular temptation.

> *The devil cannot do ANYTHING to us—temptation included—without God's permission and consent.*

Even the isolation and solitude into which the Spirit leads us to be tempted has a positive purpose. When we are tempted, God wants to be sure we are hearing His voice. He therefore allows us to be isolated from others who might otherwise exercise undue influence over us. Sometimes we confuse the voice of the Holy Spirit with the voice of someone else around us. It might be the voice of a close friend or the voice of a family member.

If people seem to be dropping out of our lives for some reason, we need not be so concerned about that fact. If you are walking with the Lord, and suddenly, for no apparent reason, someone close to you begins to develop an attitude with you or to avoid you, don't worry about it. Very possibly the Holy Spirit is taking you into the wilderness, and you are about to face a serious temptation. If many other voices were present, you might become distracted and succumb to temptation. One of the assignments of the Holy Spirit is to isolate you so that you can be alone with God.

Many of those who fall into temptation do so because of someone around them who has unduly influenced their thinking. Don't fear being alone with God. With Him, you're safe. If there are other voices in your life that are stronger than the voice of the Spirit, this is dangerous.

Relax and stop wasting time complaining about your isolation. The people who seem to be so good for us are not always as good for us as we think. If God is causing them to separate from you, let Him do it, and stop struggling against it. And when God has separated you from someone, don't go back to that relationship.

As we have seen, there is always a dynamic duo involved in the temptation process: the devil who is intent upon weakening you, and God who is using the temptation to strengthen you. The devil is intent upon driving you away from God, but God uses temptation to bring you closer to Him. The devil is intent upon breaking you down, but God uses temptation to build you up.

In the temptation of Jesus, the devil was present (and played his part), but the entire scene was orchestrated by God. The temptation of Jesus was planned in Heaven, and it was carried out by the Holy Spirit on earth. The devil was only a pawn in this entire drama. God used him to accomplish a divine purpose.

But Jesus was God, so why did He have to be tempted? Since Jesus *was* God, and God cannot be tempted, Jesus was not tempted as God, but as man. And He underwent this temptation to show us how to react when temptation comes our way too. It happened just as He was moving into His destiny, and that's the way it will happen to us too.

Jesus was tempted in several different ways, but He passed every test. Can you imagine what would have happened if Jesus had failed any of them? As a man, He had within Himself the capacity for failure. But if He *had* failed, we might not be saved today.

As I stated earlier, failing to resist a given temptation will not necessarily disqualify us for heaven, but there are some temptations that we cannot afford to fail. Too much is at stake. The welfare of others depends upon us standing strong and tall. Just as we look today to the temptation of Jesus and draw courage and strength from it, others are watching our lives, and they will be positively or negatively impacted, depending on how we react to the temptations we face.

Since temptation is *"common to man"* (1 Corinthians 10:13), those who come after us will be tempted as we are, and they will be looking to our example to see how they should handle their temptation. Therefore, every time you face temptation, you are standing not only for your own future, but you are standing for the future and destiny of others. The way you choose to respond will either encourage them to go on or, perhaps, cause them to be completely "wiped out."

During our times of temptation, therefore, we cannot afford to send the wrong message. Others must be able to see that we trust the God about whom we sing, talk, and shout. They must be able to see that the God, about whom we brag openly in public, is able to keep us from falling. For their sakes, we cannot fail; otherwise we may cause those who look to God in hope to become discouraged. If we cannot stand in the moment of temptation, we are taking steps backward, and none of us wants to go back to being what we used to be. So, we simply must stand, and God has made provision for us to stand.

If we cannot stand firm in the face of a small temptation, there is no validity to the testimony of our faith. We can no longer say that the Lord has delivered us from drugs if someone sees that we are smoking marijuana again. God is able, not only to deliver us, but to keep us delivered. He is our Deliverer, and He is our Keeper. He will keep anything that we commit to Him. As Paul wrote to Timothy, his son in the faith:

> *I am not ashamed, for I know whom I have believed and am persuaded that He is able to keep what I have committed to Him until that Day.* 2 Timothy 1:12

We are totally delivered only when we have committed everything to God. Women who testify that they have been delivered from a life of promiscuity cannot then be found to be pregnant with another out-of-wedlock baby. That testimony is one of weakness, of giving in. The Holy Spirit is always with us in our temptation, but we can refuse to hear His voice. Those who brag about walking in victory cannot afford to wind up right back in the same mess they came out of. Others are watching your life, so be more conscientious about the impact your testimony has on them.

> *Those who brag about walking in victory cannot afford to wind up right back in the same mess they came out of.*

Once you have successfully faced and conquered a given temptation, it not only gives new life to your testimony, but it lets you know that you can handle whatever the devil throws at you. With the Holy Spirit by your side, you can always out-power the devil.

Some people, afraid that their temptation signals a weakness in them, draw back from the Holy Spirit in their moment of temptation. This is a serious mistake and the opposite of what should be done to resist Satan's tricks. Stay close to God, and the devil cannot overcome you.

After you have successfully overcome a particular temptation, perhaps several times, you will no longer be tempted in that same way. Satan will then switch tactics on you, trying something else that he hopes will produce better results. But if you are unwilling to cooperate with the devil, there is nothing he can do to force you to obey him. The choice is yours. You cannot be overcome by him without your cooperation. The One who is in you is much greater than the one who is tempting you:

> *You are of God, little children, and have overcome them, because He who is in you is greater than he who is in the world.*
>
> 1 John 4:4

Since I have the Greater One fighting for me, if I lose, it's because I have chosen to lose. If I side with the weaker one, then I have no one but myself to blame for my failure. It's certainly not God's fault.

It would be foolish for me to face temptation from a position of weakness (in other words, in my own strength). If I must face Satan (and I must), it should always be from a position of strength (that is, in God's supernatural power). Why would I want to do it any other way?

One of the temptations most of us face at some time or other is the wrong use of money. Money is one of the greatest motivators known to man, and it is said that people will do almost anything for money. If we, as Christians, are tempted to accept tainted money, we have a choice to make, and I need not tell you what choice the Spirit will urge in those moments. We have the power to make the choice we wish to under the circumstances. So be careful! A failure to resist temptation affects more than you personally. When you fail to resist temptation, others will then use your failure as an excuse to fail too.

God will never consent to your being tempted beyond your anointing to resist, and if you choose to ignore your anointing and give in to temptation, you just might lose your anointing. God always provides a way of escape, but if you choose to ignore that way of escape and sin anyway, you have circumvented God's two-pronged protection for your life. By giving in to temptation, you have violated your anointing and also ignored the leading of the Holy Spirit as He gave you directions for escape. In substance, you have said to God and the Holy Spirit: "Step aside! I want to handle this for myself." And, as usual, you have made a mess of things.

Jesus' temptation came at His weakest point. He had been fasting for forty days and forty nights, and *"He was hungry"*:

> **And when He had fasted forty days and forty nights, afterward He was hungry.**   Matthew 4:2

To many it would not have seemed reasonable for the Spirit to lead Jesus into the wilderness to be tempted at His most vulnerable moment. So, why did the Spirit do that? If you don't need something or you don't want something badly enough, then how can you be tempted? Temptation hits us at the point of our needs or our wants. If something means absolutely nothing to you, there is no way you could be tempted by the offer of it, so the devil won't even try. And each of us is different. There are things that have never interested me that might be a temptation to someone else.

Jesus was hungry, desperately hungry, so that was the place the enemy first attacked Him. And he knows your weaknesses too, and will come to you at your most vulnerable moment and in your weakest area.

The Spirit also knew that Jesus was hungry and vulnerable, and yet this was the moment He chose to lead Jesus into the wilderness to be tempted. His temptation had to come at this time, because He probably could not have been tempted in any other way.

But with all of His weakness and vulnerability, temptation was not a problem for Jesus that day—or any day. He overcame every temptation set before Him. Finally, the devil was exhausted and left Him:

> *Then the devil left Him, and behold, angels came and ministered to Him.*   Matthew 4:11

In this way, the temptation of Jesus came to a close, and with the very next verse, He began His great ministry, soon preaching His first sermons (verse 17), calling His disciples (verse 18), healing His first sick (verse 23), and casting out His first demons (verse 24). From this time on, Jesus was unstoppable, but it all came about through His temptation and His resistance to that temptation.

You and I will never be able to resist demonic power in others if we are unable to overcome our own simple temptations. God has called us to deliver the sick and oppressed, to cast out demons and set people free, but how can we do that if the devil is getting the best of us in our daily lives? We, too, are called to make disciples of men, but how can we expect them to follow us when we call out, "Come," if our testimonies are not clean and sharp?

In each individual case of His temptation, Jesus turned to the Word of God for strength:

> *But He answered and said, "It is written … ."*   Matthew 4:4

> *Jesus said to him, "It is written again … ."*   Matthew 4:7

> *Then Jesus said to him, "Away with you, Satan! For it is written … ."*   Matthew 4:10

By using the sword of the Spirit, the Word of God, Jesus was able to make the devil successfully back off. If the devil continues to hang around you, it may signal that you are accommodating him. There are some people who always seem to be in sin, and it isn't difficult to see the reasons behind it. They choose to hang out with the wrong people in the wrong places, so what do they expect?

Just as we are commanded to do, Jesus resisted the devil:

> *Therefore submit to God. Resist the devil and he will flee from you.* James 4:7

In that moment, the temptation was ended, and angels came and ministered to Jesus. They were not present as long as Satan was there, for angels and devils are not compatible. Where one is, the other will not be found. When angels leave, devils come, and when devils leave, angels appear. Be sure that ministering angels feel welcome in your life.

If you tell the devil no, he has no choice but to leave you. And he leaves quickly. *"He will flee from you."* But, of course, you can't tell the devil no and see him running away unless and until you have first submitted yourself to God. When we fall in love with Him, and we begin to love His house, His people, and His Word, we will also love righteousness. It is then that we will have real power with God and be able to effectively rebuke the devil.

Some who have a lesser degree of commitment to God do a lot of rebuking, but with very little results. When you live a life committed to God, you have to do much less rebuking, for your very life is a walking rebuke to Satan.

Each of us may not truly understand temptation until we've been there and experienced it. At that moment, it doesn't feel good, and it is difficult to believe that there is some good purpose for it and that it will have a good outcome. But with each temptation and subsequent victory, we become more and more confident. We *are* in God, and we *do* have power with Him. And just as Jesus made a public display of the enemy and his cohorts, we will too:

> *Having disarmed principalities and powers, He made a public spectacle of them, triumphing over them in it.*
>
> Colossians 2:15

When faced with your next temptation—however large or small—remember its purpose. If you do this, chances are you will deal with this temptation from a whole different perspective than you have in the past.

In this regard, I sincerely believe that a time of preparation is very important for those who are called to public ministry. I recommend that they spend as much time with the Father in seclusion as possible before launching out, rather than jumping right into public life. During this time of isolation, they should allow the Lord to work on their personal lives. It is possible to be called and anointed and still not yet be appointed. The anointing will always precede the appointment, but if any man tries to appoint himself before the Father has appointed him, again, he just might lose his anointing.

> *If you tell the devil no, he has no choice but to leave you.*

Jesus allowed God the Father to work on Him during the long period from the age of twelve to the age of thirty. Having come from heaven, he lived a sinless life, but He still needed eighteen years of preparation before He could go about doing what He had been sent from Heaven to accomplish.

It was after this eighteen years of preparation that He went to John the Baptist, or the baptizer, and asked to be baptized. John protested that he needed to be baptized by Jesus, rather than the other way around. Jesus answered that it was not about either Him or John. It was about establishing a pattern for those who were to come.

Every believer must submit to someone, and Jesus submitted to John to set a precedence for those who would come after Him. It doesn't matter how anointed you are, there will always be someone over you in the Body of Christ. Those who believe that they need to submit to no one but God are sorely mistaken.

Now, let us look briefly at the specific temptations Jesus faced and how He overcame them. The first temptation He faced was to use His power for fleshly gain, to turn stones into bread because He was so hungry:

> *Now when the tempter came to Him, he said, "If You are the Son of God, command that these stones become bread."*
>
> Matthew 4:3

As we have seen, it was ordained of God that Jesus would be tempted at this point of vulnerability in His life. He was hungry and physically weak, not as strong as He normally would have been. It was at that moment that Satan chose to strike (or at this moment that he was allowed to strike), and he struck at Jesus' area of weakness.

Satan knew that Jesus was hungry, and there was nothing there in the wilderness to eat. "Just use Your power for personal gain," the enemy urged Him. The tempter, as the Bible calls the devil, was trying to get Jesus to do something wrong because of the situation in which He found Himself.

There was nothing inherently wrong with turning stones into bread, and Jesus had the power to do it. So, why did a hungry Jesus not turn stones into bread and eat them?

Temptation Does Serve a Good Purpose After All

For one thing, stones were never made to provide us with nutritional value, so turning stones into bread would have changed God's original design for them. It was not necessary for Jesus to go against nature just to prove who He was or to meet a personal need.

Your temptation may be different, but expect Satan to come at you in the most personal areas of your life. He will attack you personally, your marriage, your children, and your other important relationships. His goal is to get you to go outside of God's original plan for your life, His design for the family and for relationships.

"So what's wrong with premarital sex?" some ask. That's a very good question because it is an area of severe attack by the enemy. I will leave the discussion of the socioeconomic problems premarital sex creates for the sociologists and the emotional disruptions it causes for the psychologists. What I can say briefly is that engaging in premarital sex seriously threatens the self-esteem of teenagers, and places such a serious financial strain upon them that many never recover. But the bottom line is that premarital sex is a sin against God because it changes His design for marriage and family life.

"So what's wrong with homosexuality?" some ask. I could talk about the cultural disruptions homosexuality causes and the danger of disease it poses, but, again, the bottom line is that homosexuality is a sin against God because it changes His design for marriage and the family.

"So what's wrong with same sex marriages?" some ask. It's the same answer. It changes God's original design for marriage and the family.

As we saw earlier, Jesus used the Word of God to cause the enemy to back off from this first attack:

> *But He answered and said, "It is written, 'Man shall not live by bread alone, but by every word that proceeds from the mouth of God.' "* Matthew 4:5

Of course, the devil was not finished with Jesus. Now, he took another approach:

> *Then the devil took Him up into the holy city, set Him on the pinnacle of the temple, and said to Him, "If You are the Son of God, throw Yourself down. For it is written:*
>
> *'He shall give His angels charge over you,'*
> *and,*
> *'In their hands they shall bear you up,*
> *Lest you dash your foot against a stone.' "* Matthew 4:5-6

These verses make a very important point. Satan could not force Jesus to cast Himself from the pinnacle of the Temple; Jesus would have to cast *Himself* down. Christians need to stop using the devil as an excuse to sin. The devil cannot *make* you sin. If you sin, it's because you choose to do so. The devil challenges you, and then he sits back and waits for your reaction.

Jesus could have jumped that day, and He might even have landed safely. After all, He was and is the Son of God. So why didn't He jump? Because He knew who He was, and He had nothing to prove to the devil.

> *You don't have to jump!*

Many of us are doing unusual things just to prove who we are, but let me tell you: you don't have to jump—no matter how much of a challenge it seems to be at the moment.

Men, just because there are women working in your office who come to work half naked, you don't have to jump. Jesus had the power to resist, and you do too.

Women, you don't have to jump just because you have fallen in love with a man, and he keeps insisting that you prove your love to him. Instead of *you* jumping, tell *him* where to jump. If he doesn't have enough respect for you to leave you with your dignity intact, he's not worthy of you.

Young people, you don't have to jump to prove something or to answer a challenge. You know who you are, and you'll have plenty of chances to prove it in the days ahead. Just be yourself and let the God in you be seen. If people challenge you about who you are, it's simply because they don't know God.

Jesus resisted this temptation much as He had the first one:

> *Jesus said to him, "It is written again, 'You shall not tempt the Lord your God.' "* Matthew 4:7

That quickly ended that episode, and Satan moved on to another challenge:

> *Again, the devil took Him up on an exceedingly high mountain, and showed Him all the kingdoms of the world and their glory. And he said to Him, "All these things I will give You if You will fall down and worship me."* Matthew 4:8-9

Finally, the devil seems to have come clean. This is always what he wants—for you to bow down and worship him—and he'll promise you anything to get it.

Jesus, of course, refused. He was not about to bow to Satan, no matter what bribe he offered. And that effective ended this terrible session, because when we stand for God, He stands for us, and there is nothing the devil can do about it.

Stand strong and refuse to bow to Satan or his agents. Don't bow to the world's standards. Don't bow to quick money. Don't bow to premature progress. Don't bow to cheating, stealing, lying and promiscuous living. Don't bow to the demands of any enemy of God and His people. The same God who saved you is able to *"keep"* you in every time of trial and to present you *"faultless"* before the Father.

The apostle Jude ended his letter to the churches in this way:

> *Now to Him who is able to keep you from stumbling,*
> *And to present you faultless*
> *Before the presence of His glory with exceeding joy,*
> *To God our Savior,*
> *Who alone is wise,*
> *Be glory and majesty,*
> *Dominion and power,*
> *Both now and forever.*
> *Amen.*   Jude 1:24-25

And, to this, we say Amen as well.

Satan tempted Jesus because Jesus represented a challenge to Satan's kingdom, and that's the very same reason he tempts you. If Jesus had fallen, He would have transferred His authority to Satan, and the devil would have won. But he didn't win, and he can't win.

Take a stand against the enemy today, and prepare to say to all who know you, "Come and see. See what the Lord has accomplished in my soul through trials and tests, through afflictions, through the opposition of men, through seemingly insurmountable odds and seemingly impossible situations, and even through allowing temptations to come to me. Come and see, for He has helped me to survive the crisis and has brought me out to a place of rich fulfillment. That's more than *Surviving the Crisis.*

Make a joyful shout to God, all the earth!
Sing out the honor of His name;
Make His praise glorious.
Say to God,
"How awesome are Your works!
Through the greatness of Your power
Your enemies shall submit themselves to You.
All the earth shall worship You
And sing praises to You;
They shall sing praises to Your name."   *Selah*

COME AND SEE the works of God;
He is awesome in His doing toward the sons of men.
He turned the sea into dry land;
They went through the river on foot.
There we will rejoice in Him.
He rules by His power forever;
His eyes observe the nations;
Do not let the rebellious exalt themselves.   *Selah*

Oh, bless our God, you peoples!
And make the voice of His praise to be heard,
Who keeps our soul among the living,
And does not allow our feet to be moved.
FOR YOU, O GOD, HAVE TESTED US;
YOU HAVE REFINED US AS SILVER IS REFINED.
YOU BROUGHT US INTO THE NET;
YOU LAID AFFLICTION ON OUR BACKS.
YOU HAVE CAUSED MEN TO RIDE OVER OUR HEADS;
WE WENT THROUGH FIRE AND THROUGH WATER;
BUT YOU BROUGHT US OUT TO RICH FULFILLMENT.

I will go into Your house with burnt offerings;
I will pay You my vows,
Which my lips have uttered
And my mouth has spoken when I was in trouble.
I will offer You burnt sacrifices of fat animals,
With the sweet aroma of rams;
I will offer bulls with goats.   *Selah*

COME AND HEAR, all you who fear God,
And I will declare what He has done for my soul.
I cried to Him with my mouth,
And He was extolled with my tongue.
If I regard iniquity in my heart,
The Lord will not hear.
But certainly God has heard me;
He has attended to the voice of my prayer.

Blessed be God,
Who has not turned away my prayer,
Nor His mercy from me!   **Psalm 66**